SURVIVAL KIT
FOR TEACHERS AND PARENTS

SECOND EDITION

SURVIVAL KIT FOR TEACHERS AND PARENTS

SECOND EDITION

Myrtle T. Collins, M.A.
Assistant Professor of Education
University of Hawaii, retired

Susan J. Benjamin, M.A.
English Department Chair
Highland Park High School
Highland Park, Illinois

 GoodYearBooks

An Imprint of ScottForesman
A Division of HarperCollins*Publishers*

GoodYearBooks

are available for most basic curriculum subjects plus many
enrichment areas. For more GoodYearBooks, contact your
local bookseller or educational dealer. For a complete catalog
with information about other GoodYearBooks, please write:

GoodYearBooks
ScottForesman
1900 East Lake Avenue
Glenview, IL 60025

Library of Congress Cataloging-in-Publication Data
Collins, Myrtle T.
     Survival kit for teachers and parents/Myrtle T. Collins. Susan J. Benjamin—
2nd ed.
          p.   cm.
     Includes bibliographical references (p.) and index.
     ISBN 0-673-36035-0
     1. Classroom management—Handbooks, manuals, etc. 2. School disci-
pline—Handbooks, manuals, etc. 3. Human behavior—Handbooks, manuals, etc. 4. Child rearing—Handbooks, manuals, etc.
     I. Benjamin, Susan J. II Title.
     LB3013.C55 1993
     371.1'02—dc20   92-43037
                                                                      CIP

Book Design by Melissa Cutting Ackermann, Highgate Cross+Cathey
Copyright © 1993 Myrtle T. Collins and Susan J. Benjamin.
Copyright © 1975 Scott, Foresman and Company.
All Rights Reserved.
Printed in the United States of America.

ISBN 0-673-36035-0

2 3 4 5 6 7 8 9 - MH - 01 00 99 98 97 96 95 94 93

To the memory of my late husband DWane, my cherished life partner for over fifty years, to my daughters, Beth and Anne, and to my grandchildren, Monica, Deborah, Lia, Jonathan, and Mackenzie, who are very special to me.

M.T.C.

To my husband Marc, and my children, Brad and Lindy, who inspire me every day, and to my nurturing parents, Howard and Jane.

S.J.B.

PREFACE

Providing the best possible education for children is a major concern, both to society and to the dual communities of teaching professionals and those being served. The atmosphere—the learning climate created by teachers and parents—is crucial to how students feel about learning and to what extent they can and will achieve learning objectives. The greatest amount of learning often takes place when teachers and parents cooperate and collaborate with one another to create a positive learning environment. The suggestions in this book are designed to enlarge the learning community, to help both teachers and parents augment positive behaviors and alleviate stressful situations so that learning can be the focus of schooling.

Survival Kit for Teachers and Parents, Second Edition, reflects the dramatic societal changes of the last few decades. In addition to time-honored concerns of teachers and parents, this book contains subjects that were previously unknown or unmentionable in polite circles. It combines one of the most complete, practical student-behavior reference lists ever compiled with pragmatic, easy-to-implement suggestions for action.

If you're picking up *Survival Kit* for the first time, turn to the list of Beliefs on page viii, which sets the tone of our approach and helps you become acquainted with the philosophy behind this book. After that, you'll find *Survival Kit* easy to use. The table of contents lists 162 behaviors frequently found in school-aged children, and the index at the back of the book supplies helpful cross-references.

New teachers, veteran teachers, teacher-trainers, counselors, administrators, and parents can all benefit from the information in this book. Each behavior includes a summary, or "capsule," that describes the behavior. Immediately following each capsule are "options," which provide concrete alternatives for dealing with the behaviors. We have not attached a priority value to the sequence of the options, nor is any one of them a finality. Instead, each option is introduced with a verb, and the entire list is alphabetized by the introductory verbs. Choose the option or options that works best for the individual student or your situation.

The Appendix defines further a number of techniques that are referred to throughout the "Options." These are listed in alphabetical order for easy reference. And finally, we've provided an annotated bibliography of additional resource materials for those of you who wish to read in greater detail about current educational issues and student behaviors.

ACKNOWLEDGMENTS

Survival Kit for Teachers and Parents first came on the market in the mid-1970s. Now, nearly two decades later, we present an updated version to carry our readers into the year 2000 and beyond. This edition reflects the dramatic changes currently taking place in schools and in society as a whole.

We are indebted to many people: teachers of much experience; student-teachers and their supervisors; parents; thousands of children; school administrators; University of Hawaii colleagues; fellow authors; and helpful librarians. In particular, we would like to thank professional staff members of Township High School District 113 in Highland Park, Illinois, including Arnold Barbknecht, Jane Gard, Glen Hartweck, Sheldon Schaffel, Dianne Schmidt, Mary Swanson, Luis Vazquez, and Jim Warren, for their invaluable advice, support, and expertise. We are also appreciative of medical information provided by Dr. Anne Bronner and Dr. Eugene Isaacs. Finally, we gratefully acknowledge our publisher-advisors at GoodYearBooks, Acquisitions Editor Tom Nieman and Developmental Editor Roberta Dempsey.

Myrtle T. Collins   **Susan J. Benjamin**

Beliefs

The authors of *Survival Kit for Teachers (and Parents), Second Edition,* believe that:

1 Teachers and parents are intelligent and are able to respond positively to suggestions as well as to innovate ways of working with children. (Many of the techniques described in this book will serve as reminders of techniques once used or will show that other professionals and parents agree with an approach.)

2 Teachers and parents already have a repertoire of successful strategies to help students learn.

3 The brunt of creating a positive classroom climate rests on the classroom teacher. School administra-tors, parents, and the surrounding community help set a positive tone in which education can flourish.

4 No one technique works for all students all the time. A given technique may indeed be ineffective with the same student the second time around.

5 The best disciplinary measures open to the school community are preventive ones.

6 The school has the capability of organizing a case conference procedure, sometimes including only the teaching staff and principal, and possibly including counselors, social workers, psychologists, nurses, physicians, and reading specialists.

7 A student's misbehavior is a signal, an SOS—for the teachers, administrators, and parents who are in prime positions to administer aid.

8 To help a child the adult must honestly feel that the child is asking for help and can indeed be helped.

9 The wise teacher does not confuse academic evaluations with discipline.

10 The best approach to helping people is to explore the reasons for particular behavior patterns and then to explore alternative choices for effecting change.

11 No behavior is by chance (the principle of causality) and each is, therefore, significant.

12 The humane teacher's goal is to find ways of working with students that will produce the greatest benefit and will enhance self-esteem and personal dignity.

13 Because every student is unique, ways of working with each student will be unique.

14 Whatever is done reinforces behavior one way or another.

15 Disruptive behavior in a social context carries with it inevitable consequences.

16 Utilization of extrinsic rewards in modifying behavior does not prohibit the student's chances of developing high intrinsic values.

17 The teacher's conduct provides a model for how students are expected to behave. Student and teacher behavior are highly related and reflective of one another.

18 The teacher's ability to work effectively with individuals is challenged and complicated by the fact that the individual is a member of a group and that the group is affected by the treatment of the individual members.

19 Teaching a child how to learn is more important than teaching a child what to learn.

20 Consistent behavioral expectations are of prime importance in establishing and maintaining an atmosphere conducive to learning.

21 Our swiftly changing world dictates an approach to discipline more flexible and pragmatic than ever.

22 No learning is singular and pure; rather it is a composite of facts, skills, and attitudes.

23 The optimal goal of educators and students is self-discipline.

24 Participation and responsibility are prerequisites to self-discipline.

25 A person who thinks well of himself or herself will exercise self-discipline.

26 Teachers and parents who have their own values clarified are better able to help students work through conflicts and confusion.

27 Children cannot learn well when they are embarrassed, ashamed, or under a great deal of stress. Therefore, parents and teachers must create a learning atmosphere in which the norm is positive reinforcement and all members of the learning community show respect for one another.

28 In order to achieve optimal effectiveness, school personnel should work closely and collaboratively with the families and communities of those they serve.

Appendix

ABRASIVENESS

SEE ALSO
Acting Out
Talking Out

CAPSULE: Abrasive personalities rub us the wrong way and make us want to scream or set our teeth on edge to such an extent that we find ourselves trying to avoid close contact with them. One person may be abrasive because of pompousness, another because of a rasping voice that never ceases, another because that person does not exemplify what he or she exhorts others to do—and that person is always exhorting! Some describe their most abrasive acquaintance as "one who has all the answers." Coping with abrasiveness is like chasing a phantom, but perhaps some of the following will at least help you live with the abrasive one in your classroom.

OPTIONS

1 Allow students to feel they have some control over the situation—perhaps by drawing up a simple agreement that focuses on diminishing the abrasive behavior.

2 Analyze reasons for a student's abrasiveness. This means getting to know something about his or her abilities, experiences, background, and physiological and psychological drives and consulting those best qualified to help. For instance, a speech teacher might help the student with a voice problem.

3 Anticipate and check the undesirable behavior with a diverting comment. ("Jim, you were about to _____.")

4 Ascertain whether the student patterns the behavior

after someone. Then talk to the student about the effect this "imitation self" has on others.

5 Ask yourself questions such as the following: Does the student's abrasive personality really interfere with the student's or others' performance? Am I magnifying the effect the abrasiveness has on the group? Should I talk this over with another teacher to gain some perspective? What kind of attention is the student seeking? How much does he or she deviate from the norm?

6 Assign responsibilities that require attentiveness and merit praise—preferably solitary activities in a strategic location.

7 Group the abrasive one with students who can help. Your sixth sense must tell you whether to place the student with the quiet, thick-skinned students who will put up

with the behavior or the testy, vocal group that will tell the abrasive student why he or she rubs them the wrong way. If you choose the latter, be ready to move in with dispatch and capitalize on your information: "Mary, I couldn't help overhearing the group putting you down because you upset their work by

_____. Let's talk about that sometime when you drop by after school."

8 Make brief notations of the child's abrasive behavior. Does a pattern appear?

9 Reinforce nonabrasive behavior, making no mention of abrasive deportment.

10 Try using bibliotherapy (see Appendix). Several prominent athletes and politicians are accused of being abrasive; perhaps stories about them may give the student some insights.

ABSENCES *DURING TESTING*

CAPSULE: Teachers can become very testy about having to accommodate students who miss exams! School administrators, aware of the inconveniences incurred by absences at such times, often help by systematizing make-up schedules. If the make-up testing is left to the discretion of the teacher, the following suggestions may be helpful.

OPTIONS

1 Arrange for private testing, mutually agreeable to you, students, and others.

2 Communicate with parents so that they are aware of examination dates and the student's attendance record. Make sure that parents understand test policies and procedures.

3 Establish a make-up policy whereby the student takes the initiative to make up the exam.

4 Formulate, *with the class,* the procedure that will be followed throughout the year with regard to make-up tests. Establish limitations and consequences that are fair. Be sure that students are not penalized for circumstances beyond their control.

5 Give an oral examination. (This provides an excellent opportunity to get to know the student better.)

ABSENCES *FOR RELIGIOUS REASONS*

CAPSULE: Apart from national holidays (Labor Day, Fourth of July, etc.) observed throughout the year-round or nine-month school year, religious holidays are dictated by a person's faith. Some families are stricter than others within their own denomination.

O P T I O N S

1 Accommodate students who will be absent for religious reasons by planning ahead before the absence about how they will handle make-up work.

2 Handle the absence as excused if prior requests have been made by the parents or guardian.

ABSENTEEISM

SEE **ALSO**
Truancy

CAPSULE: Absenteeism and truancy are not synonymous. Truancy connotes idleness and conscious, willful absence of a sporting nature, while absenteeism is simply excessive absence for any number of reasons, ranging from school phobia to parents' demands that the student stay home to help with the family's business. Often the problem is related to sickness and finances. Most schools, for liability reasons, have established procedures for recording and reporting absences, and can survey and analyze each student's pattern of attendance.

Chronic absentees soon distinguish themselves among faculty and students. If illness is not the cause, a high number of absences probably indicates a potential dropout. One thing is sure, the student needs some help because the consequences of long periods of absence are major, even for the ablest scholar.

O P T I O N S

1 Confer with the absentee regarding the real reasons he or she chooses to stay away from school. ("Bill, it's pretty clear that staying home is more pleasant than coming to school, because your mom is gone and you can watch TV all day.")

2 Discuss the absentee in a staff meeting (see Appendix). The pooled information may be used to construct a behavior change program for him or her.

3 Individualize and personalize the absentee's instruction so that long periods out of school take less of a toll.

4 Work with parents, the student, and other school professionals (a counselor, if available) to develop a plan ensuring the student's regular attendance.

ABUSED CHILDREN *OVERTLY*

SEE ALSO
Abused Children, Sexually

CAPSULE: Although the extent of child abuse in our society is impossible to know, much has been written about the significance of the problem in the past few years. According to some studies, the highest incidence of child abuse occurs among boys in grades one through six, after which the greatest incidence is among girls. Speculation regarding the factors that give rise to child abuse include (1) a long-standing pattern of physical abuse, stemming from a parent's upbringing, (2) substance abuse in the home, and (3) rising costs of living and the frustrations of feeding and clothing a family.

The child who comes to school with welts on his or her body, who hangs around before school or after everyone else has gone home, or who speaks of beatings at home may be an abused child. The quiet, subdued, frightened child may be the object of abuse, too, but that child's deportment is less arresting. As you become acquainted with your students, you may catch hints of abuse. The following ideas suggest possible courses of action if there is an abused child in your class.

O P T I O N S

1 Assign an abused child to an older student of the same or opposite sex (see Junior Counselors, Appendix). If abused by his mother, for instance, a youth may need a satisfying relationship with another female so that he doesn't feel all women are bad. The junior counselor can function as a confidante and/or a surrogate parent.

2 Deal with the child in a friendly, caring manner. Your warm, fair approach may convince him or her that not all adults are cruel child-beaters.

3 Help the student judge adults in perspective, including the one who beats him or her: "List ten things adults do that annoy you; list ten things adults do that please you. By each item put the initials of the person you immediately identify with that thing. Now make statements that include the item listed, plus a 'but' statement, such as, 'I am annoyed (or I hate) being beaten by _____, but I like him when he's not drunk'." *Note:* Such an exercise can be used with a group or on an individual basis.

4 Initiate contact with the parents of the abused child, not to complain or scold them, but to get acquainted. Most parents who violently abuse their children refuse to come to the school. They may ask for help in coping with their child. Be prepared to recommend information sources, such as parent-education courses and free or inexpensive counseling on handling problems with children.

5 Report the case to the proper authorities. Consult your administrator for advice regarding the procedure to follow. Most, if not all, states now have reporting laws.

6 Use sentence completion (see Appendix) to learn the child's feelings. (My mother always . . ., My father is . . ., Adults are . . ., My stepfather . . . .) *Caution:* Use this technique judiciously: remember, you are not a moralizer or a judge. However, knowledge of how the child feels toward adults can be helpful in dealing with the problem.

ABUSED CHILDREN *SEXUALLY*

SEE ALSO
Abused Children, Overtly

CAPSULE: In recent years, the pernicious problem of sexual abuse has come into public view and requires level-headed handling. Sexual abuse can take two forms. *Overt* abuse leaves visible scars, such as black eyes, broken bones, or damaged organs. *Covert* abuse deposits scars via vitriolic verbiage, subtle hostile deeds, or secretive, threatening, clandestine encounters. The crime of sexual abuse, a covert act, occurs in every social stratum and in all racial groups.

The average age of the sexually abused child is eight. Accurate statistics are virtually impossible to obtain, but some estimate that 10 percent of the children in the U.S. are sexually abused before they reach the age of eighteen. Generally, the abuser is known to the child; often the abuser is a family member or a close friend. While the common belief is that girls are more often victims than boys, some studies contend that male victims report the incidents less frequently.

Dealing rationally and sensibly with the problem is extremely difficult. Because sex is such an intimate, private act, sexual behavior is a touchy subject for parents. Discussing normal, healthy sex with a child is tough. Parents resist discussing aberrational sexual behavior with their children for fear of creating warped ideas and feelings about sex.

Unfortunately, sometimes the most trusted person, a parent or other close relative, is the offender. *Incest,* sexual contact with a person who would be an ineligible partner because of blood or close family relations to the victim, can leave the victim with feelings of "impurity" throughout life.

Schools are in a unique position to participate in preventive efforts to make children aware of the lures offenders use, including promises of anything from candy to a job.

OPTIONS

1 Arrange for repeated inservice training of teachers on the subject. Participate in the development of an awareness training program concerning child sexual victimization in your school district. The program should cover the following areas: (1) information regarding offenders and victims, (2) a thorough review of your school's response to the law that requires people in the helping professions who have reasonable cause to believe that a child is suffering serious physical or emotional injury to report the situation to the appropriate authorities, and (3) a thorough review of the available community resources such as crisis centers and child abuse prevention services, the local department of social services, the police department, and services offered by local churches and synagogues. Each of the above will be able to supply you with a wealth of current literature on the subject.

2 Become informed regarding strategies to prevent sexual molestation. Help children express their feelings without reservation and learn to say no to aggressors including family members. Encourage children to select a certain individual to whom they can go for help.

3 Contact the public library if you know of a good reference book that should be on the shelves. Periodically procure from the library a complete list of books that deal with sexual abuse. Refer children and parents to library resources.

4 Refer the child (and parents) to health professionals. Start with the school nurse and the child's pediatrician. Work jointly with other professionals to identify and treat the problem. A social worker or psychologist may also need to become involved.

5 Remember that you may be the best friend and the only confidante of the sexually abused child. Allow the victim to count on you, but don't feel you have to have all the answers. (See number 4 above.)

6 Use bibliotherapy (see Appendix).

ACCIDENTS

SEE ALSO
Clumsiness
Hyperactivity
Stress

CAPSULE: Accidents occur now and then no matter how many precautions are taken. Yet, studies show that accidents don't "just happen." They are *caused,* and nine out of ten could be avoided if adequate safety measures were taken.

In the home, chains of events place extra strain on families, increasing the possibility of accidents. The same may be said for the climate of a classroom. Playgrounds, science labs, hallways, stairs, and school buses are all places waiting for an accident.

Most accidents happen when children are tired, hungry, hyperactive, rushed, frightened, worried, upset, or under stress. And Saturdays and Sundays are days for the accident-prone to be extra cautious.

O P T I O N S

1 Become acquainted with the accident-prone child's family circumstances. Worry over a sick parent or a family move could be distracting.

2 Check the safety of the school facilities and share your awareness with the students: "We have been bringing snow into the halls today so they're slippery."

3 Consult the school nurse regarding any child who is frequently having accidents. Is vision a problem? Can he or she hear well? Is the student poorly coordinated?

4 Examine all students' health folders at the beginning of the school year. Insist that school administrators share all knowledge of special health conditions with you.

5 Hold a safety consciousness week. Encourage students to share their understanding of safety concerns through essays, posters, cartoons, jingles, and plays. Contests generate interest.

6 Post first-aid information bulletins in a conspicuous place in the school office and in the classrooms and review them periodically. Include emergency telephone numbers.

7 Remember that young people are curious and likely to handle anything within reach simply because it's there.

8 Set the tone and tempo of the school activities so that "making haste slowly" is the watchword, not "hurry, hurry, hurry."

ACNE

SEE ALSO
Health Problems
Self-Concept

CAPSULE: Although the disease is not limited to adolescents, acne often has its onset during teenage years. Acne is generally caused by hormonal changes within the body. Poor general health and psychological stress may exacerbate the problem. Usually, acne clears toward the end of adolescence. The teacher can help the acne sufferer in a variety of ways.

O P T I O N S

1 Invite the school nurse or other health professional to talk to students about a variety of concerns, including acne.

2 Recommend that the student consult a dermatologist.

3 Show films on proper care, diet, and exercise for healthy skin.

ACTING OUT

SEE ALSO
Hearing Problems
Insubordination

CAPSULE: Acting out is aggressive, overt behavior precipitated by covert feelings. Although acting out is common among elementary-school students and usually reaches its peak around age nine, it is not restricted to that age level. Consider the behavior a symptom of something that needs attention, and accept it temporarily while you consider the following questions: Is the student being rejected by peers, and, for this reason, acts out? Is the acting out telling something about the *group*, as well as about the particular student? Is this "just a phase" that the student is passing through? How much does this behavior really interfere with this student's and others' performance? Are you being consistent and self-disciplined? (Vacillating behavior on your part can actually prompt acting out!) Are you motivating the students or manipulating them? Is the acting out a result of a behavior disorder? These and other questions will help you gain a proper perspective.

Having conducted your personal inquiry, turn your attention to other matters. Pay attention to attitudes expressed in nonclassroom matters (conversations with friends, notes, scribbles on notebooks). Recognize the law of readiness in dealing with the student. Take care that privileges are not hastily and heatedly withdrawn—most people have long memories where hasty, unfair action is taken.

Finally, remember that withdrawal of a certain privilege, in an effort to change a pattern of behavior, often intensifies the aggressive misbehavior, so if you feel your theory is sound, don't flinch. "Things get worse before they get better" is often applicable where acting out is concerned. It may be the student's last gasp in an effort to foil divorce from his or her gratifying old patterns! Since acting out is among the chief concerns of teachers, a rather exhaustive list of options is offered.

OPTIONS

1 Act on the behavior. Ignoring the problem may intensify it in addition to allowing classroom distractions for other students.

2 Agree with the student upon a silent signal that can serve as a deterrent. ("O.K., Jenny, after this when you start to act out I won't say anything to you in words, but I'll quietly place an eraser on its end on the blackboard tray.") A nod or a smile can do as well.

3 Agree with the student upon certain times when his or her kind of acting-out behavior may be acceptable.

4 Allow the student sufficient opportunities to release tension. ("Max, would you help Mr. C. lift those boxes?")

Give the student an opportunity to be important in the class.

5 Anticipate and divert acting-out behavior with a question, a chore, or a command. ("Maria, were you about to make a contribution?")

6 Ask the child to "occupy this space." There is something ominous about one's body filling a designated space! Better that than "Sit down and shut up!"

7 Avoid definitive statements like, "Marta, you're *always* acting out." Instead, try, "Marta, I've been noticing what a good sport you've been in gym lately."

8 Avoid responding with anger or sarcasm, which only reinforces the notion that the method works. Rather, react with "I" messages. "Judy, I feel very upset when you do that."

9 Combine consequences and rewards. ("Jim, you know we don't permit shoving others in line, so please take your place at the end. When we have all gone into the auditorium, will you please close the door and turn out the lights? Thank you.")

10 Confer with such important people as the parents, former teachers, the school nurse, physicians, and counselors. Study available school records, then act according to your best judgment. (See Staff Meeting, Appendix.)

11 Confer with the student in a private environment, conveying the idea that it is the behavior, not the stu-dent, that is unsatisfactory. It is highly important for the teacher to be clear about the goals to be sought. At the close of the conference the teacher should be able to recap what has been learned and to state what the next step should be. A minimal plan of action should be clear to both, and a specific plan for assessment should be set up. Conferences should help students realize that they are responsible for their own behavior.

12 Consider denying certain privileges, but offer alternatives; then be aware of opportunities to reinforce improved behavior. Make sure the child is not denied the very activity he or she needs most, as in, "O.K., since you've been acting out so much today, no P.E.!"

13 Control the student's environment with established limits that offer security but that afford some latitude for being himself or herself. ("Susan, I know you're very upset, but dropping the books and throwing the chalk are not appropriate here, so take these erasers outside and clean them by knocking them against the post. Thank you.")

14 Establish, with the class, logical consequences for behavior. State them to all students, verbally and in writing, so that everyone understands a common code of conduct.

15 Examine the seating arrangement. Try seating the student away from others who are easily distracted or who may act out.

16 Isolate the student in a nearby place so that you and the rest of the class can get on with the lesson. Be sure the class members understand why the student is being isolated. Caution: There is always the possibility this treatment is exactly what the student wants.

17 Keep brief anecdotal records of the student's behavior and review them periodically with someone you trust, such as a fellow teacher, a school counselor, or a doctor.

18 Note, and remember for future reference, the things that seem to trigger acting out. Is the student worse when classmates bring things from home to share? When the parents of other students visit class? When a field trip is planned?

19 Praise the student about something that carries the inference he or she is competent, not just behaving well. ("You have a lot of manual dexterity, Jim; a lot of boys would have dropped that huge pile of plates before getting to the counter.")

20 Remind the student, firmly and in a friendly manner, that what is acceptable elsewhere is not acceptable here.

21 Resort to prescribed supension. This means the student can stay in school as long as he or she behaves, but overstepping certain bounds means being sent home. The student thereby virtually writes his or her own ticket.

22 Send the student to the main office, as a last resort. Caution: When transferring the problem to another authority, make sure that person has some information upon which to act, possibly in the form of a note.

23 Use mediation (see Appendix).

24 Use peer pressure. ("Mary is not quite ready; when she is, we'll go to the puppet show.")

25 Use positive reinforcement.

ADOPTED CHILDREN

SEE ALSO
Bilingual Children

CAPSULE: With changing family patterns, adopted children are not a classroom rarity. Understandably, some adopted children fantasize a great deal about "Who am I?" especially if their roots and background are not explained to them satisfactorily. In school, adoptees often compare notes on their lots in life and provide mutual support.

In classroom or playground interactions, during "power plays" or other activities, children often attack others in areas of vulnerability. No matter how well parents have informed them or how much love has been lavished upon them, adopted children feel their "differentness." Childhood cruelty may come out as taunts of "You have no mother; you have two mothers; your *real* parents didn't love you—they gave you away."

The best antidote for doubts and upsets with regard to adoption is a delicate balance between assurance of affection and some ready ways to cope when questions arise. Adopted children often feel comfortable discussing concerns with a teacher. For this reason, you should acquaint yourself with the family and its composition. (Are there siblings? What are the ages of the parents? Are there other adopted children?) Perhaps some of the following suggestions will be helpful.

O P T I O N S

1 Discuss the child's school experiences with the parents. Strategize about ways to help the child deal with peer teasing and potential rejection. Encourage parents to discuss adoption openly with their children. Children should be armed with information about themselves *before* they attend school. Learning about aspects of adoption from any source other than parents can be devastating to a child.

2 Encourage the adopted child to talk freely about his or her role in the family. Be discreet. Baiting children into sharing anxieties, without the skill to heighten and broaden their value judgments, is not only damaging, but also unprofessional. Be mindful that the adopted child has the same need and right as any other child to question, challenge, and resist parents' guidance.

3 Give the student opportunities to relate the story of his or her adoption through forms of expression: stories, poems, songs, drawings, scrapbooks, and photographs, for example. Young children often enjoy sharing the story of their childhood with a class; older children may consider it a private matter.

4 Seek help from a school social worker or an outside agency. Professionals are trained to explain the adoption process in positive, understandable terms. Also, through role playing and other techniques, professionals can encourage kindness, empathy and positive interactions among all students.

5 Show the child by your attitude that you not only think that *he* or *she* is special, but that *all* children are special.

AGGRESSIVENESS

SEE ALSO
Abrasiveness
Anger
Argumentativeness
Temper Tantrums

CAPSULE: Aggressive behavior, both verbal and physical, is on the increase among students. Classroom management is threatened by this phenomenon, as is the juvenile justice system. The aggressive student is combative and filled with obtrusive energy. Some typical expressions of aggressiveness are disregarding the rights of others; pushing others around or manipulating them to fulfill one's own needs; being sarcastic, insulting, or belittling to others; and making demands rather than requests.

Aggressive people may achieve their desired goals but they do so at a high cost. The student runs the risk of rejection by peers, conflict with teachers and parents, and possible academic failure. Additionally, the aggressor elicits from associates either passive submission or a "fight-back" reaction. In either case, the aggressor is a loser.

OPTIONS

1 Acknowledge the slightest increment the student makes in modifying aggressiveness.

2 Channel the student's energies into hobbies and sports.

3 Establish a trusting relationship with the student and eventually urge him or her to modify aggressive behavior in a step-by-step program.

4 Work with the school counselor or other professionals to determine whether the student should receive a special education screening. An undiagnosed learning disability or behavior disorder will often lead to aggressive behavior.

AIDS

SEE ALSO
Health Problems
Sexually Transmitted Diseases

(ACQUIRED IMMUNE DEFICIENCY SYNDROME)

CAPSULE: AIDS is an extremely serious, usually sexually transmitted, viral disease involving a breakdown of the body's immune system. Not everyone with AIDS is diagnosed because some are carriers while others develop AIDS-related complex (ARC) and exhibit symptoms such as swollen lymph nodes and fever. Many ARC victims will develop AIDS.

Adolescents and adults contract AIDS through sexual contact, drug injections, or blood transfusions. Young children can contract the disease at birth through an infected mother or by receiving a contaminated blood transfusion.

To date, authorities believe that evidence suggests AIDS is not communicable through normal contacts in a school setting. The human immunodeficiency virus (HIV) that causes AIDS lives in body fluids, especially blood and semen. Because the virus is usually transmitted from body to body through direct fluid contact, transmission in a school setting is improbable.

OPTIONS

1 Adopt a school policy for dealing with the afflicted student or teacher.

2 Become informed about the disease by reading reports published by the U.S. Department of Education and the U.S. Department of Health and Human Services.

3 Consider the legal aspects of dealing with AIDS students. (Under law, schools may be forced to allow AIDS victims to be educated in "the least restrictive environment.")

4 Consult your school nurse and social worker when you have questions.

5 Don't be surprised if the victim is angry. Try to redirect that anger toward non-self-destructive behavior. Cite familiar role models.

6 Make sure the school has safe disinfectant procedures for handling blood or body fluids.

7 Maintain an up-to-date file of information about AIDS.

8 Offer a course on sexually transmitted diseases for faculty and students. Include explicit units about safe sex and "safer" sex. Make sure that students understand the possible consequences of sexually irresponsible behavior.

9 Provide counseling for the AIDS student. Be willing to be the liaison while the student is absent from school.

10 Remember the AIDS-infected child's right to privacy.

11 Take stock of your own attitudes toward AIDS victims. How is your empathy? What messages are you sending to your other students?

12 Work with support systems in the community. Consult the Centers for Disease Control (CDC) for guidance.

ALIBIING

SEE ALSO
Forgetfulness

CAPSULE: Alibis are pleas of negligence intended to convince the listener of the speaker's good intentions. They are intended to relieve the speaker of behavioral consequences. Alibis take many forms such as pleas for attention, protestations of helplessness, or sympathy requests. Alibiing students have constructed well-set patterns, so experiment with ways to rescue them.

OPTIONS

1 Counsel students, with emphasis on collecting clues to their problems. Do the alibis usually involve certain people (mother, sister, friend)? Do they proliferate at special times (before tests, during bad weather, after vacations)?

2 Discuss cause/effect relationships and the logic of accepting consequences for behavior. (See Class Discussions, Appendix.)

3 Establish an out-of-school relationship with students to see how they handle themselves away from the classroom. For example, invite a student to attend a community function with you. Is the student punctual or late with a ready-made excuse? Use a student's conduct as the topic for a future one-to-one conference.

4 Give clear assignments with deadline dates and well-defined consequences for defaulting. Class agreement on suitable consequences will give this tactic some weight.

5 Help the student identify the causes of his or her habit. ("Think of three things that delay you in the morning and of one solution that you could try tomorrow.") Listing the ideas on a note pad and giving it to the student adds dignity to the counseling session. A simple agreement (see Commitment Technique, Appendix) might be a natural result of the conference.

6 Telephone the parent, in the presence of the student, to assess the validity of the alibi. This could bring about an instant cure!

ALLERGIES

**SEE
ALSO**
Health Problems

CAPSULE: The allergic student is a wary one, sometimes miserable and unable to function in the classroom, especially if exposure to chalk dust, hidden ingredients in the school lunch, or the pollen of trees, grass, and weeds in the school environs causes the recognized symptoms: red and itchy eyes, nasal congestion, wheezing, or hives.

The diagnosis of allergies has been quite well established in recent years. The treatment of allergies, however, is lagging, though slowly gaining ground. At the same time, more and more people are claiming allergic afflictions. This may be due, at least in part, to increasing levels of pollutants in our environment.

The substance that causes an allergy is called an *allergen.* (Common allergens are mold spores, house dust, and animal hair.) Researchers have found that allergies are activated by a serum protein called IgE antibodies which are attuned to specific allergens.

Contact with those will cause the release of *histamine*, which in turn causes the symptoms of the allergic disorders mentioned above. These antibodies are detected in various ways, most commonly by skin tests.

People who suffer from asthma and hay fever receive relief using the standard antihistamines or shots prescribed by their physician. Sometimes hives can be traced to a specific food, drug, or airborne substance.

While cases are rare, teachers need to be aware of the allergy to stinging insects, particularly to honeybees. A bee sting causes sudden pain, and the poison produces swelling. Some people are so sensitive to bee stings that they are in danger of dying if not treated immediately.

O P T I O N S

1 Acquaint yourself with the telephone numbers of poison control centers, doctors, and hospitals.

2 Ask the school nurse to post a list of the students who are in jeopardy because of certain allergies.

3 Remember that insect stings should be taken seriously. Get the entire stinger out immediately. Keep the student quiet and inactive. Place cold compresses on the bite to reduce the swelling. Be prepared to use CPR (cardiovascular pulmonary resuscitation) or find someone who can.

ANGER

CAPSULE: Anger is a strong emotion that everybody knows quite well. It can be useful, as well as destructive. The challenge is not one of eliminating anger altogether, but of dealing with it, and using the energy generated by it in positive ways.

Recognize the symptoms of anger: flushed face, taut throat, and tears, for example. Be aware that anger usually occurs as a result of failure to accomplish a goal, of feelings of inferiority, abuse, or guilt, or of having had something taken. It may represent legitimate rebelliousness toward unfair, intolerable conditions.

When students are angry, they need a listener who is cool-headed. Adding your anger to the scene won't help. From what they report, make a mental note as to whether it was one person or a group that riled the student. Deal with anger in private, if possible. Allow students sufficient time to sulk, cry, or retreat before expecting them to return to the group.

O P T I O N S

1 Develop, with the student, a mentally rehearsed plan of action to put to use if a similar incident recurs ("When she makes me angry again, I'll . . . ."). (See Class Discussion, Appendix.)

2 Discuss the psychology of anger in class. Help students recognize the phenomenon as a part of their personality that can be useful when controlled. "Let's begin by listing things that make most people angry. Now list specific things that make you angry. Now let's work in small groups and talk about ways to cope with anger."

3 Encourage the student to practice stating his or her anger using first person, rather than second or third. ("*I* am so angry," instead of "*You* [*he, she*] made me do this!")

4 Have the student list ten things that made him or her angry during the past week. An analysis of such a list

might help the student see that he or she must be responsible for his or her own behavior.

5 Remove the student from the situation. Give the student "cooling off" time. As soon as possible, meet with the student to discuss the anger. Maintain a calm and dispassionate manner during the discussion. As an empathic listener, help the student discover personal resources with which to deal with anger.

6 Role play, shortly after the fact, an incident involving anger. (See Role Playing, Appendix.)

7 Tell the student how you cope with your anger. ("I have two major ways of coping with my anger. Do you want me to tell you about them, or do you want to see if you can figure them out as the semester goes along?")

ANXIETY

SEE ALSO
Fearfulness

CAPSULE: Anxiety can best be described as uneasiness. A moderate degree of anxiety serves as a splendid motivator; an excessive degree immobilizes.

Common comments of an anxious person are, "I have butterflies in my stomach," "My hands are sweating," "My head is splitting." The familiar ring of such comments indicates the universality of the emotion. Conspicuous in the areas of jobs, sex, and school, anxiety is impelled by desires to succeed or avoid failure; the closer people hover near perceived failure, the more likely they are to behave recklessly. Lack of structure and fear of the unknown generate anxiety. Quarrelsomeness and pressure outbursts are common symptoms of anxiety in adults.

Sometimes anxiety is caused by school-related pressures. Often the causes of anxiety are not manifest, and all one sees are the symptoms, such as tics, blinking, subvocal throat clearing, hair twirling, sucking, and the like, all of which are distress signals and safety valves.

As a teacher, expect to deal with anxiety in many forms. Your sensitivity will eventually sharpen your awareness to the stresses that emit anxiety signals, and you can respond professionally and helpfully.

OPTIONS

1 Acknowledge the student's creditable gains in dealing with an anxiety-causing situation. ("Mr. Field tells me you handled your fear of the water with real courage today.")

2 Acquaint yourself with the history of the child's anxiety. (Examine cumulative records; consult former teachers and parents.)

3 Anticipate the fears of the student and share your appreciation of his or her anxious feelings. Encourage the student to speak openly. ("Claudia, I know you worry about the report to your parents, so why don't we go over it before it goes to them?" or "Since you get so anxious about taking tests, let's talk about some test-taking strategies.")

4 Ask another teacher to observe the anxious student. Discuss your mutual observations. Analyze what you might be doing (unintentionally) to exacerbate the situation.

5 Ask yourself how much you feel the anxious student deviates from the norm. To what extent are you more aware of that student's behavior than that of others? In other words, are you overreacting?

6 Change activity or routine, if possible, when anxiety symptoms become evident.

7 Check the level of difficulty of the academic material you are using. Consider the goals of the student as established by you, the parents, and the student. Are they realistic?

8 Consult a counselor, psychologist, social worker, or the school nurse, who can suggest proper referral procedure.

9 Keep anecdotal records of the situations that make the child most anxious. (Dec. 1, 19—: Danny came to my desk three times this morning, asking if he would have to take the swimming test today. Dec. 3, 19—: Danny went to the washroom and a classmate reported that he had vomited. When he returned to the room he was pale and the first thing he asked me was if he would have to take the swimming test, since he had been sick. Dec. 8, 19—: The following boys forgot their swim trunks at home: Dick, *Danny*, and Sam.)

10 Observe the student's out-of-class behavior with friends during free periods, at lunch, and so forth. You might pick up a clue to his or her anxiety.

11 Seek opportunities to enhance the student's self-image. ("We were all proud of you for finishing your speech, even though you were brave enough to share with us the fact that you were nervous.")

12 Use the student's name often, kindly, and without threat.

ARGUMENTATIVENESS

SEE ALSO
Attention Seeking
Talking Out

CAPSULE: Healthy argumentation livens up a group and enhances the thinking process, but is sometimes uncomfortable for teachers, parents, and other students. Perhaps this discomfort is tied to a long-held notion that there must be a winner and a loser in every intellectual skirmish. The skillful teacher can minimize competition while encouraging openness to a variety of ideas.

Arguers usually come on strong. They may have learned the control power of arguing. Some arguers are intellectually motivated; others are merely cantankerous. All are talkers who enjoy disputes and debate. They may be amusing, cocky, overbearing, or threatening, but they are *not* evil! The student in your class who always wants to argue could be the key to a memorable semester—with your judicious guidance.

OPTIONS

1 Allocate certain times in your class schedule for argumentation. This way students can anticipate those times and other tasks will not be jeopardized.

2 Ask the argumentative student, on occasion, to write the arguments, instead of speaking them. Have another student react to the arguments.

3 Focus the student's attention on improving his or her logic and judgment and away from always winning an argument. ("Next time the umpire calls a foul, Ted, try to imagine yourself in his place.")

4 Require the student to preface at least some statements with, "I agree with you on___." He or she may need experience in seeing that others also have sound ideas.

5 Speak candidly about the arguer's penchant for overwhelming the other students with argumentativeness. Suggest that the arguer might enjoy those mental gymnastics even more with added participation of others. Constantly listening to one's own ideas can become quite dull!

6 Use the Ann Landers technique (see Appendix).

7 Work on listening skills. Quiz the arguer on his or her ability to understand someone else's point of view.

ASHAMED STUDENTS

SEE ALSO
Anxiety
Self-Concept
Withdrawn Children

C A P S U L E : Shame is more than loss of face or embarrassment. It is an inner sense of being completely diminished or insufficient as a person. It is the self judging the self. A moment of shame may be so humiliating, so painful, that a person feels he or she has been robbed of dignity and exposed as basically inadequate, bad, and even worthy of rejection. Without maturity and perspective, students may become immobilized by shame and learning may be hampered.

O P T I O N S

1 Analyze students' behavior in terms of responses to embarrassment. What rolls off one student's back nearly kills another. Why?

2 Confer one-to-one with the student. Provide examples of others who have lived with shame (such as well-known abuse victims). Try to elicit the causes for shame.

3 Enlist the help of the counseling and guidance staff for acute cases of shame.

4 Make special efforts to help the student come to the realization that he or she has worth. ("You do _____ better than anyone I know.")

ASSEMBLY DISRUPTION

CAPSULE: Large-group activities generate human turbulence. Therefore, develop a tolerance for a normal amount of noise where large groups are involved. Anticipate what might cause an eruption so that you can be prepared to handle it. Remember to look upon negative conduct as a symptom of something that deserves attention, not something that should be taken personally by you. Be aware of the "high intensity" times in school (just before a tournament, before holidays, at times of conflict between groups of students or students and faculty, for instance) and adjust your level of tolerance accordingly.

Begin assemblies by establishing a proper atmosphere. Use an opener that commands attention (such as singing the national anthem or the school song). Likewise, use an appropriate closer (dismissal by the student body president, for example). Establish a tone, through your own deportment, that is conducive to acceptable behavior and that emphasizes standards of conduct instead of school rules. *If* all the props, audiovisual aids, and so forth are in readiness for the assembly, *if* the physical climate of the auditorium is correct, *if* teachers are seated among the students (instead of in a huddle in the rear), *if* you have circulated and periodically reviewed acceptable assembly conduct, and *if* the content of the assembly is worthwhile, problems can be avoided.

OPTIONS

1 Assign helping roles to potential disrupters, such as controlling traffic or distributing programs.

2 Avoid unnecessary confrontation and embarrassment for a first offense. Chat with students after the assembly about why they were disruptive. Share your disappointment and communicate your belief that they will be positive audience members next time.

3 Communicate nonverbally with students during the assembly by establishing eye contact and gesturing.

4 Involve students in planning and executing the next assembly.

5 Move near the disruptive student and remain there until all is quiet. If necessary, invade the student's space and place a hand on his or her shoulder.

6 Prepare students to attend the assembly. Role play good listening behaviors in class. Discuss listening techniques and why listening is important.

7 Remove the disrupter from the audience with an explanation of why he or she is being asked to leave. Refer the student to the principal or a school disciplinarian.

AT-RISK STUDENTS

SEE ALSO
Absenteeism
Disabilities, Learning
Dropouts

CAPSULE: Students "at risk" are those who, if not identified early enough and helped to get on track in school, will likely drop out and get into severe trouble. Research points to three major groups of students that fall into this category: (1) the high absentees, (2) the poor achievers, and (3) the lonely or friendless. Add to this information the fact that up to 30 percent of our nation's youth fail to finish high school and the incidence of suicide among this group is on the increase.

According to studies, school failures and truancy or absenteeism are significant predictors of adult behavior. Therefore, extra attention given to helping "at-risk" students succeed in school may help them to become more successful adults.

OPTIONS

1 Be especially mindful, on a day-to-day basis, of the lonely, the absentees, and the underachievers, and don't give up on them. You may be their only hope for the day.

2 Conduct a learning assessment on the at-risk student.

At-risk students often have special educational needs.

3 Encourage your administration to think through and establish a policy that addresses at-risk students in all grades.

4 Look to the counselor in your school to provide leadership for the development of prevention programs in the elementary school. Potential dropouts can be spotted as early as the third grade.

5 Work with parents to ensure that students' basic needs are met. Are students fed and clothed adequately? Do they have appropriate school supplies?

ATTENTION DEFICIT DISORDER (ADD)

SEE ALSO
Attention Span, Brief
Hyperactivity

CAPSULE: Individuals with Attention Deficit Disorder cannot handle normal stimulation and for them, positive stimulation becomes negative. Students with ADD respond to their overstimulation in a variety of ways. Some withdraw into escape worlds; others exhibit a great deal of physical movement in an effort to connect with the stimuli at hand. Because of their poor on-task behavior, students with ADD are often misunderstood and misdiagnosed as underachievers, immature, or behaviorally disordered.

Students with ADD experience difficulty focusing in learning situations. Typical behavior might include staring out a window during a lesson instead of looking at the teacher, or leaving a seat during a lesson to wander around the classroom. Experts believe that up to 10 percent of children, three-quarters of them boys, have attention deficit problems. Some outgrow or learn to compensate for the disorder. Above all, remember that Attention Deficit Disorder is a medical condition and can be diagnosed by a physician.

OPTIONS

1 Discuss some of the child's behaviors with the school nurse, psychologist, and/or social worker. Identify strategies to help the child, such as preferential seating or removal of stimuli.

2 Discuss the student at a staff meeting (see Appendix).

3 Recognize this child as the one who can't sit still and is always finding an excuse to be on the move.

4 Refer the child to a doctor for diagnosis. Attention Deficit Disorder is a medical disorder and can sometimes be treated with medicine.

5 Seat the child close to you. Remind the child nonverbally (hand on shoulder, etc.) to focus on the lesson.

ATTENTION SEEKING

SEE ALSO
Loneliness
Tattling

CAPSULE: Every student needs attention, seeks it, and gets some. However, some students seem positively gluttonous in their desire for attention. Teachers may have difficulty in quelling the whistler, the hummer, the giggler, the wisecracker, the whisperer, the swearer, the gossip, the clown, the crier, the dawdler, all of whom are saying, "Look at me! Listen to me! Pay attention to me!" Try to help attention-seeking students understand how they are trying to control those around them. You may be amazed at their insight. What they are doing may be quite all right—in small doses. Good humor and skill in recycling the students' energy will make them less demanding and you more serene.

O P T I O N S

1 Provide cooperative learning opportunities (see Appendix) in which the student can work closely with and gain attention from peers.

2 Talk to the child privately about his or her ways of asking for attention. The student may not be aware of the impact of the behavior. Between the two of you, devise a check plan that will help the student realize the extent of the attention-getting behavior. ("Jeff, I'll bet you don't realize that you ask to borrow things at least five times every day, and I believe it is your way of getting my attention, because your exams show that your memory is really good. Let's talk." Note that Jeff's memory was praised at the same time that a corrective measure was suggested.)

3 Use the child's name kindly and often. This provides a modicum of attention, and the student may not seek much more.

ATTENTION SPAN *BRIEF*

SEE ALSO
Anxiety
Attention Deficit Disorder
Eye Problems
Health Problems
Hyperactivity

CAPSULE: Teachers and parents often mention the child with a "short attention span," rarely realizing that, for the level of material and conditions prevailing, perhaps his or her span is as good as can be expected.

Brief attention spans may be related to physical discomforts (vision and hearing problems, hunger, or fatigue) as well as to the academic material at hand. Your job is to provide attention-engaging learning experiences and tasks that are commensurate with students' abilities and learning styles.

OPTIONS

1 Allow the student some choice in the order of the subjects he or she will study.

2 Ask the student to run an errand for you after completing the current task.

3 Become a master at knowing when to accelerate, decelerate, change activities, raise or lower your voice, place your hand on the child's shoulder, and so forth. Know when to "recharge" the student just enough to maintain his or her attention. Vary activities within a lesson.

4 Reinforce younger students with a token (see Extrinsic Rewards, Appendix) for every five minutes of attention. Allow the student to trade the tokens for objects of his or her choice at the end of a determined time. Gradually withdraw the extrinsic reward.

5 Remind students of what they had hoped to accomplish in a given time. This may encourage attention to a task for a little longer. ("Monica, you wanted to have this birthday card finished for your mother by noon.")

6 Show the inattentive student precisely how to do better. ("Pat, you are bogged down in this problem because you made a little error in subtraction here.")

BAITING THE TEACHER

SEE ALSO
Deviousness
Insurbordination
Note Passing

CAPSULE: Students sometimes enjoy the game of "Baiting the Teacher." Usually the student's attitude and facial expressions belie his or her intent, but the clever student can lay a subtle trap for the unwary. Good humor and honesty in conducting your class are better antidotes to baiting than playing a continuous game of one-upmanship. If the teacher engages in one-upmanship, everyone loses. The art of questioning is a sound and profitable form of preparedness for the "baiter."

OPTIONS

1 Confront and surprise the baiter. ("Jim, you're baiting me. We're all quite aware that you already know my stand on the subject of _____. However, in the past month I've modified my views somewhat. Can you guess how?") This approach openly settles the matter of baiting, without rancor. At the same time, it engages the student in a guessing game that few can resist.

2 Ignore the baiting and thereby extinguish the student's ploy through lack of reinforcement.

3 Respond to a question with a question. (Student: "Mr. B., why do you question the right of _____ to _____?" Teacher: "Why shouldn't I?")

4 Submit to the student, in private, the possibility that he or she uses baiting more to impress classmates than to befuddle the teacher. If a student concedes the correctness of this analysis, the student will have interpreted his or her own conduct, and the behavior will undoubtedly diminish.

5 Tell the student, privately, that he or she is making only partial use of one of the best tools for becoming a success—astute question asking. Suggest that insincerity and preoccupation with trapping someone may be spoiling the inquiry mode. If you are sincere, the student may record your advice for future, if not present, use.

BILINGUAL CHILDREN
POTENTIALLY ENGLISH PROFICIENT

SEE ALSO
Self-Concept
Transient Children

CAPSULE: Many frustrations spring from classes that include non-English-speaking minorities. The concept of "equal opportunities" is really put to the test in such classrooms. However, the teacher who is willing to approach the challenge with an open mind and a good measure of empathy can provide a wealth of opportunities for multicultural sharing.

Resist the temptation to expect students who are learning English as a second language to be totally enamored of all that is new in their school and country. They're probably frightened and overwhelmed. Don't be surprised if children coming from a highly structured school system begin acting out when they find themselves in a more liberal setting. They are responding to a form of culture shock. The most common behavior problems generated by non-English-speaking students fall in the areas of acting out and withdrawing, both dramatic indicators of frustration.

O P T I O N S

1 Build the ego of the child by using his or her name often in connection with a simple request. ("Zi Ping, please turn out the light.")

2 Contact the family of the child for suggestions about how to bridge cultural gaps. Assure the family you are interested in them and their child.

3 Exhibit good work of the child and samples of good efforts.

4 Give the student an assignment to become the teacher and teach classmates some of his or her native vocabulary. Note: If you, the teacher, will learn some key words in the language of the bilingual child, that child can teach you how to say them and you will become learners together. Speaking to the students in their native language (at least a few words) can help build their self-esteem.

5 Pair the new student with one who knows the language and reward the tutor for the gains made by the non-English-speaking student. Rewards might include a special outing for tutors or a congratulatory letter or plaque.

6 Teach about the native country of the new student. Introduce English words that sprang from his or her native tongue; show artwork from the student's country; tell stories of successful people from his or her culture; show films of that country.

7 Teach meaningful concepts and give the student practice in grasping the concepts in many different ways. For example, teach the multiple meanings of a certain word or idiom (such as train, train of thought) through dramatization, visual aids, or tactile experiences.

8 Use bibliotherapy (see Appendix). A child can identify with a famous literary character from his or her own culture who was also confronted with adjusting to a new country and a new language.

BITES *ANIMAL*

CAPSULE: Nearly a million humans are bitten and treated for animal bites each year. Dog bites are the most common, but cats, squirrels, raccoons, monkeys, foxes, rabbits, rats, mice, and others might pose a threat.

　　Pets in the classroom or laboratory should be carefully monitored even if they are caged or on a leash. The animal may be carrying tetanus germs even though you feel there is no chance of rabies.

OPTIONS

1 Be strict about the rules that must be adhered to when dealing with animals.

2 Build lessons in basic skills around information on animals, highlighting kind and proper treatment. Keep in mind that most animals are wild and therefore unpredictable in behavior.

3 Check the student's file and/or contact the student's physician regarding allergy information and specific treatment recommendations.

4 Remember that the animal that bit the child must be kept under observation for ten days, so do not kill the animal.

5 Report any nip or bite to the school nurse immediately. In the absence of the nurse you should wash the wound gently with a mild soap and water. As soon as possible, report the bite (and circumstances surrounding it) to parents.

BLUFFING

SEE ALSO
Self-Concept

CAPSULE: Bluffers know they are not going to succeed forever. Bluffers are the great pretenders, the stallers for time, the fantasizers. In the classroom, they pretend to know the answer when they don't, to have more information than they in fact have, and to have skills that they haven't. "Insecure" describes them. Bluffers have a poor self-image. They are more brash and outspoken than the habitual liar, with whom they differ in that the bluffer is pretty sure that if he or she can delude someone (teacher, parent, classmate) just this once, he or she can correct the deficiency and no one will be the wiser. A characteristic comment is, "I bluffed my way through that class, but now I'm really going to study." Bluffers need help in sound ways of learning and retaining information so that they won't feel compelled to bluff.

OPTIONS

1 Allow the student to save face, but also let on that you know he or she is bluffing. ("You are skimming the surface of a good point, Marc, but how well have you thought the problem through, really?")

2 Call the bluff. ("Barbara, you and I both know that you are not prepared to perform the experiment, so why don't you stop bluffing?")

3 Tell the student, in private conversation, that you've noticed that that student pretends to have read and studied so much more than he or she obviously has. Let the bluffer know that you can help him or her cope successfully with lessons, thereby eliminating the need to bluff or pretend. (See Study Skills, Appendix.)

BLURTING OUT

SEE **ALSO**
Compulsiveness
Talking Out

CAPSULE: Blurting out can be disruptive, noisy, incongruous, and attention getting. This annoying behavior should be curtailed for the sake of the learning of the rest of the class.

OPTIONS

1 Ask well-phrased thought questions instead of simple recall questions.

2 Help students select some restrainers to assist them in controlling the blurts. ("Every time you blurt out, write the time on this card that has your name at the top. We'll use a new card every day, and at the end of the week maybe we can detect your pattern. Perhaps you have a better idea.")

3 Locate students who lack impulse control strategically in the classroom, close to the front of the room or to the teacher. Use proxemics to control impulsive behavior by periodically standing close to the student or

gently placing a hand on a shoulder as a reminder to exercise self-control.

4 Mix directed with nondirected questions to involve everyone verbally and to discourage blurting out. Vary the format, recognizing both students with hands up and students who do not volunteer and need to be drawn into classroom discussion.

5 Set the tone (and rules) for the class at the beginning of the year. Recognize only those students who respond appropriately and wait for recognition. Discuss with students the need for "processing time" before they speak.

BODY ODORS

SEE ALSO
Halitosis
Health Problems

CAPSULE: The sense of smell is easily fatigued. When in the vicinity of fecal, urinary, and ordinary body odor, most people have little tolerance. Offensive body perspiration odors generate withdrawal from the source. Even though applied psychologists have made our society so B.O.- and cologne-conscious that "the sweat of our brow" is in jeopardy of extinction, body odor problems persist.

Our responses to smells are not only deeply imbedded in our culture, but are also quite resistant to change. The person who emits a bad odor because of a lack of bathing or clothes washing has a simple problem to solve, but the people whose body chemistry works against them can rightfully despair. The malodorous ones in the classroom will be one type or the other. In either case, they ought to be dealt with delicately so that the problem can be resolved with self-esteem intact. Try to avoid embarrassing students when dealing with such a personal, sensitive matter.

O P T I O N S

1 Ask the physical education teacher or counselor to assist the student.

2 Consult school health specialists. They will find tactful ways to approach the immediate problem, as well as the underlying cause.

3 Emphasize awareness of the body—its beauty, its capacity for change, and its care. ("Toni just got a new motorcycle and I see her polishing it and taking very good care of it. Would you say you take as good care of your body as you do your motorcycle, Toni?")

4 Present a hypothetical case to which students can react. ("I once had a boss who had such strong body odor

I could scarcely be in the same office with him. What would you have done?")

5 Show videotapes on proper body care and hygiene.

6 Talk directly, honestly, and privately with the student who has a body odor problem. ("Jim, everybody has problems and I'm taking the liberty today of talking to you about one of yours. Occasionally your clothes smell bad. Do you have a clue as to why this might be?")

7 Talk to the student privately about appearances. ("In order to look fresh, you must be fresh. That means bathing and brushing teeth daily.")

BOREDOM

CAPSULE: Boredom has become an excuse for not performing a given task. The statement "I'm bored" is potent because it has accusational and intimidating overtones. To be a party to boredom means one is not stimulating, motivating, or exciting. If your students speak of boredom or reflect boredom in their attitudes, consider the following questions: Are the assignments nearly always the same? Are you overdoing programmed materials? Do you require an excessive amount of memory work? Are you rehashing old stuff on a too-easy level? Are you talking too much? Have you included the students in the planning at all? Are you concerned too much with fixed, pat answers that have no emotional quality, and not enough with imaginative, contemplative thinking? Do you really value student interest, or are you primarily interested in picking up your paycheck? When was the last time your class witnessed your being excited about an idea? If you have to think hard to answer these questions, you may have your number-one clue to your students' boredom.

O P T I O N S

1 Allow the class members to feel that they have some control over the situation. ("This lesson can be conducted in a number of ways: by lecture/exam; cooperative learning, peer editing, a study/project approach, or traditional daily assignments.") (See Flight Plan, Appendix.)

2 Capitalize on the interests and talents of the students when teaching basic concepts. ("We've observed that the different amounts of water in the glasses produce different tones. Jenny [the bored, musically talented one], will you reproduce the vocal tone of each glass as you strike it?")

3 Provide puzzles, word games, and art supplies that are available for use without special permission.

4 Surprise the students with an unexpected activity. ("I promised you a quiz on *Hamlet* today, but instead we're going over to Mr. Johnson's house across the street, and Juan Martinez, who is now playing Hamlet in summer stock, is going to talk with us about the role." Or, with primary students: "Instead of using workbooks today, as we usually do, let's take a walk and see how many things we can find that are oval, round, triangular, square, or rectangular.")

5 Vary activities to appeal to diverse learning styles and right- and left-brain-hemisphere-dominant learners. Lessons should include combinations of visual, auditory, and tactile stimuli. (See Learning Styles, Appendix.)

BULLYING

SEE ALSO
Aggressiveness
Anger
Self-Concept

CAPSULE: Bullying is common among children, and unless the pattern is checked or replaced it continues into adulthood. Because bullies are often loud-mouthed and large, they can scare off the weak and intimidate those who hang around. Most likely, bullies are compensating for their own fears. The bully needs polite, consistently firm role models. In your classroom or school you can curb bullying by providing ground rules that define conduct expected of all students. (These rules will work better if the students have a part in formulating them.) Carefully consider some immediate and long-range efforts to help bullies; these could range from deliberately separating students physically from those they bully to guiding their understanding of such behavior on an intellectual level.

OPTIONS

1 Combine a reprimand with a dignified command. ("Josh, stop bugging Luigi and bring me the science kit from the round table.")

2 Discuss the bully in a staff meeting (see Appendix) with or without the student present. Try to pinpoint his or her fears and create positive reinforcement strategies.

3 Discuss the problems of bullies with the class. Present a hypothetical or real case for discussion, such as, "A few years ago I had a student who delighted in bullying those smaller than himself. One day . . . ." (See Class Discussions, Appendix.)

4 Help the bully interpret his or her own behavior.

("Jason, the movie we saw showed bullies who wanted attention, bullies who wanted to get even with someone, and bullies who wanted to show who was the boss. Which one did you feel you understood the best?") Then, proceed to establish a strategy to follow the next time the student feels like playing the role of the bully. Use his or her ideas instead of yours.

5 Help the student to understand anger. Counselors use several strategies to help students cope with aggressive tendencies. One is to have bullies sign "contracts" that establish the areas in which they ought to change.

Another is to pair aggressive and passive students one-on-one to work through a given problem, using guidelines established by the group.

6 Reinforce the student's good behavior with an observation that may come as a surprise to him or her. ("Nick, you treated that little girl so gently after she fell off her bike!")

7 Role play (see Appendix). The bully may, for instance, play the role of the one who is bullied. Avoid preaching. Let the activity speak for itself. The bully may, for the first time, appreciate what such behavior causes another to feel.

BURNOUT

SEE
Stress **ALSO**

CAPSULE: Although every generation has faced pressures, technological advances, information overload, drug availability, and the changing family structure have created an entirely new set of stressors for contemporary school-aged children. Students accustomed to viewing problem-solution or happy endings in thirty-minute television sit-com time slots look for instant gratification in their own lives. Additionally, high-school students face enormous academic pressures as they look toward selective post-secondary options and challenging college board exams.

Many students want to try everything, be in everything, excel in everything . . . today. When pressures seem overwhelming and expectations are unmet, students may lapse into a malaise, a tired depression often called burnout.

O P T I O N S

1 Encourage the student demonstrating symptoms of burnout to talk to a doctor or to have a complete physical examination. Symptoms of burnout are similar to those of a number of diseases.

2 Talk to parents of students who seem headed for burnout. Together parents and teacher(s) can strategize about ways to alleviate stress.

3 View videotapes on the subject of burnout. Conduct class discussions (see Appendix) on realistic expectations and dealing with stress.

4 Work on decision-making skills with students. Help students prioritize their extracurricular activities and other commitments.

BUS CONDUCT

SEE **ALSO**
Dangerous Conduct

CAPSULE: The school bus is one of the more energy-efficient ways to transport students to school. The bus also provides a vehicle for student socialization. Without guidelines and definite behavioral expectations and models, student socializing can become raucous and even dangerous. The school can enhance bus safety by setting down and sharing guidelines with students and parents before the school year begins.

OPTIONS

1 Confer privately with involved students when an incident occurs. Ask the right questions to redirect anger. ("Can we list some ways to cope with the problem?") This eliminates taking sides and hurling insults. It also reduces the teacher's temptation to moralize or become vindictive.

2 Consider having parents of students who disobey rules ride the bus on a rotational basis.

3 Create a bus committee that includes school personnel, parents, and students. Involve representatives of all constituencies in writing and disseminating the rules. Having representation will help constituents "buy into" the rules.

4 Establish a hierarchy of treatment for unseemly bus conduct.

- *First offense:* Hold a conference including the bus driver, the student, and a school official.

- *Second offense:* Hold a conference including the bus driver, the student, a school official, and a parent.

- *Third offense:* Hold a conference including the student, a school official, and the parents to consider the student's removal from the bus for a stipulated period of time.

5 Use brainstorming (see Appendix) for generating solution ideas among the students. Remember, no ideas are rejected!

6 Use student monitors with prescribed responsibilities mutually agreed upon by students, school administrators, and parents.

CARD PLAYING

SEE ALSO
Gambling

CAPSULE: Card playing has invaded many schools on an epidemic scale. When card playing interrupts instruction, it can be defined as a problem.

If card games are a nuisance in a classroom, there is probably some deficiency in the teaching or the course content. Administrators can render support to teachers by arming them with a well-publicized policy statement regarding card playing. Teachers can plan a wide variety of activities to keep students productively engaged so that students will have no time for card games. Cards consume time, so unless one has time to spare, card playing can become a student's occupational hazard.

OPTIONS

1 Be supportive of existing regulations and still enlighten the students regarding democratic avenues for making changes (student council, petitions, and so forth). Even though the outcome may not be favorable to the card players, they will feel that at least they were heard and will be made aware of the consequences of card playing. If the verdict is favorable, they will have the satisfaction of having experienced a proper procedure for effecting change through the democratic process.

2 Discuss card playing in a class meeting. You might begin with questions such as, "What is the place for card playing in the school setting?" or "Is it possible to play cards without getting hooked on them?"

3 Have the card players maintain records of how they spend their time for one week. If card playing is conspicuously cited in the record, and grades, health, and work are suffering, the students need guidance in planning better use of their time.

4 State your position regarding cards. ("There will be no card playing in this class.") Communicate with parents so that together you can reinforce the undesirability of card playing in school.

CARELESSNESS

SEE ALSO
Forgetfulness
Vandalism
Wastefulness

CAPSULE: A common complaint of teachers and school administrators is that the students are careless about the equipment and materials in the school. They are careless about library books, about the amount of supplies they use, about littering, and about the care of the buildings in general. Furthermore, reproaches are often met with "I-don't-care" responses. Similarly, parents are hard put to control the loss of sweaters, baseball mitts, tennis shoes, racquets, and so on. Lost and found departments in schools are known to have enough unclaimed goods to start a well-stocked thrift shop.

In the face of attacks from teachers and parents, and not knowing the value of things, children take one of two routes. They feign or feel indifference, or they dissolve into penitent tears. In the former case, the adult is likely to respond with belligerence and threats, and in the latter, with overindulgence and overprotection. Neither is good for the child. The best approach is to teach children that logical consequences follow careless acts. The consequences are sometimes uncomfortable, even painful. Adults must be strong enough to avoid enabling behaviors and to allow young people to accept the consequences of carelessness.

OPTIONS

1 Avoid preaching, scolding, or nagging when carelessness is the problem. Point out the condition the careless act has caused.

2 Be friendly but firm about the fact that the student must face up to the consequences of his or her carelessness. ("I'm sorry, Rachael, that you left one of your tennis shoes on the bus, but there is no way to get it now and there are no extra shoes, so you'll have to sit on the sidelines today.") Parents who rush to the store for another pair of shoes are teaching the child that carelessness is not detrimental; they perpetuate the very behavior they say they want to eliminate.

3 Find opportunities to praise the student for his or her improved attention to the care of things. ("Jill, I've noticed how much better you've been taking care of your books and the things in your locker lately.")

4 Use common sense about entrusting something of extremely high value to a young person, such as sending a collector's item with a child to school. Losing or damaging it might incur the wrath of adults. Assume the responsibility yourself, thereby conveying the value concept as well as your willingness to share the rare object with others. Values are absorbed; they are not forced.

CARSICKNESS

CAPSULE: Car or motion sickness is often a problem with children and can be disruptive on field trips. If a child has a history of this unpleasantness, that child will probably alert you. You can then place the student at the front of the bus or see that he or she takes some medication prescribed by the family doctor. Don't dispense any medication on your own!

O P T I O N S

1 Ask parents to share with you any special needs or precautions of which you should be aware prior to the first field trip. Send a note to all parents requesting such information.

2 If children are susceptible to motion sickness, take common-sense precautions. Don't be too surprised to find a clever young one who claims the affliction just to be able to sit in the front of the bus!

3 Take some plastic bags with you, just in case.

CHANGING FAMILY STRUCTURE

SEE ALSO
Acting Out
Rejected Children

CAPSULE: According to recent reports, approximately 50 percent of all children will spend some time as part of a single-parent family. This change in the traditional family structure may give rise to custody tugs-of-war, which are then resolved in court based on the best interests of the children.

Caught in the middle, children are relatively help-less, though they do have the right to an attorney. Young school-aged children respond with feelings of fear, helplessness, and abandonment caused by the missing parent. Older children (9-12) have the same feelings, but are also angry and may reject one parent. Adolescents (13-18) feel loss and anger and tend to "act out" through generally aggressive behavior.

Consumed by their priorities, both parents hope that the children are sufficiently resilient and tough to survive the separation and loss of one parent from the home without too many scars. The Family Educational Rights and Privacy Act of 1974, a federal law, entitles mothers and fathers to have access to school records, regardless of custody or residential arrangements.

OPTIONS

1 Ask to see and place in the child's file any legal documentation regarding custody changes.

2 Become acquainted with any siblings in the school. They may have different surnames.

3 Familiarize yourself with the school's policy regarding the release of the student to adults other than the parent who enrolled the child. Become familiar with housekeepers or nannies and their levels of authority in the home.

4 Handle discussions and assignments relating to single-parent homes and children whose parents share custody with tact and understanding. Adapt curriculum and classroom resources to include various family types and structures.

5 Maintain a complete list in the school office of children and custodial parents.

6 Request that parents provide information regarding custodial particulars: Which parent is to receive report cards and other notifications?

CHEATING

SEE ALSO
Deviousness
Fearfulness
Grades

CAPSULE: Cheating is a product of pressure. It is not enough to say "Everybody does it—so what?" The fact is that not everybody does it, though cheating does occur to an alarming degree throughout our schools and universities. Students cheat for many reasons—some to compensate for a physical disability, some to compensate for failure to study, and some to compensate for a poor memory, but all because they are afraid. A system that overvalues acceptance in "the best schools" or that prizes a letter grade over competence to perform a task plants the seed of its own destruction, and widespread cheating has proved to be the consequence.

In order to minimize the practice, discuss the psychology of fear and how it manifests itself in times of stress. Teach and practice with students valid study skills to empower them to achieve on their own and to alleviate pressure. Create a positive classroom climate and convey the attitude that you expect your students to exhibit integrity. Here are some specific things you can do to reduce students' temptations to cheat and to restore positive attitudes toward any kind of evaluation.

OPTIONS

1 Ask the student to contribute the questions for the exam. ("Next week's exam will be composed of questions formulated by you students. Work in pairs and submit two recall (memory) questions, two hypothetical problems, and two evaluative questions.")

2 Assign grades based on alternative or "authentic" assessments (see Appendix). One form of alternative assessment is a portfolio in which students keep their written work and projects. In addition to teacher evaluation of their progress, student evaluation is a key component in portfolio assessment. Students assess their work and choose which samples should be included in their final portfolios. Using alternative assessments (as opposed to standard assessments—tests) gives students an opportunity to be reflective about their own progress. Alternative assessment may also de-emphasize competition with others, which can lead to cheating.

3 Consult with others, such as a counselor or other teacher, who can help you work with the student who needs self-confidence bolstered.

4 Control the testing environment by moving the furniture and separating students who "help" each other. Move inconspicuously toward would-be cheaters to curtail their efforts.

5 Discuss the problem with the cheater privately. Learn how he or she can be freed of the need to cheat, then experiment with some of the ideas the two of you discussed. ("Pat, you say written exams scare you to death and that your dad insists that you get good grades, so you feel forced to cheat—even though you know it's dishonest. As a result of our conference, we've agreed to administer two kinds of tests for awhile —the regular written one and an oral one, with the higher grade going on your record.")

6 Give credit, where applicable, for the process as well as for the final answer.

7 Give open-book or group-participation exams. The former emphasizes skills other than rote memory, and the latter emphasizes a cooperative approach to problem solving.

8 Give some oral exams, where cheating is more difficult.

9 Use alternative versions of a test so that students sitting next to one another have different sets.

CHEWING TOBACCO

SEE ALSO
Drinking
Drug Use

CAPSULE: In addition to hard drugs and alcohol the use of chewing tobacco has crept into the culture. Some responsibility has to be laid at the feet (or plate!) of popular sports heroes whose "cool" image has grabbed the identification of youth.

Clearly, those who hanker for the stimulation of tobacco juice have never seen themselves wiping the drippings onto the sleeve of their shirt or pondered the impact of discolored teeth and pungent breath.

OPTIONS

1 Educate students, through reading materials, visuals, and class discussions, about the dangers of chewing tobacco, especially cancer of the mouth and throat.

2 Enlist the aid of the athletic director or coach to prohibit the use of chewing tobacco during practice or play.

CLIQUES

CAPSULE: To many students, being part of a clique spells security. Inclusion may be subtly or openly based on religion, race, or social mores. Students often slip in and out of various cliques. Be prepared to lend a shoulder to the bruised student who is rejected from a clique.

OPTIONS

1 Discuss values with students and try to interest them in analyzing feelings about being included or excluded. Such an exercise may clarify students' thinking and alter their feelings.

2 Lead the entire class into a discussion of cliques and their *raison d'être.*

3 Read or produce plays that deal with being in or out of a clique. The students can write their own scripts.

4 Use role playing (see Appendix) to help students identify with the feelings of being left out of the group.

SEE
ALSO
Attention Seeking

CLOWNING

CAPSULE: The class clown might very well be your most misunderstood student. His or her conduct says, "I want attention; I know how to get it, but I'm also worried about what others think of me, and I'd like to be taken seriously." All of this is hard to believe when the rascal has sabotaged a perfectly good plan and temporarily stripped you of control.

For a starter, ascertain, if you can, who the clown's model is. Then consider his or her strengths that could be affirmed with a natural diminution of the clowning. Instead of the easy put-down, try for some shrewd understanding of why the student needs to clown so much. Clowns usually live up to the expectations of their teachers. If you opt for sarcastic warnings, expect to herald encores.

Examine objectively such management details as seating arrangement, your mode of handling routines (roll call, lunch count, and so on), and the class schedule. Above all, scrutinize the pace of your teaching approach. One can actually promote disruptive behavior by being disorganized or insensitive to the flow of activities. Revamping classroom routines may be simpler than trying to break a class clown's behavior patterns. Finally, you will have to decide whether the student is a clown or a real troublemaker, in which case you may need outside help.

OPTIONS

1 Give the clown responsibility that demands concentration. Find an isolated place for the student to work. The task should make him or her feel important and indicate that you take the student seriously. ("Fred, these science cards are all mixed up and they need to be sorted before Mr. K. calls for them. A few are missing, so please place the numbers of the lost ones on the board. Thank you.")

2 Interpret the clown's goals for him or her. ("You crave attention and you feel clowning is the best way to get it. How else might you get attention?")

3 Laugh with the clown but refrain from overdoing your appreciation; the latter makes the other students impatient with your overindulgence and doesn't help the clown. It's better to be direct and make the limitations clear. ("That moment of levity should brace us for the seriousness of the next few minutes. Get ready for your quiz.")

4 Praise the student about something that carries the inference that he or she is sensitive, not just a clown.

("Mary, your clowning around is fun for all of us in moderate doses. I'm glad to see you establish your own limits.")

5 Preempt and redirect the student's disposition to clown. ("Anne, you act as though you have a good idea brewing. Tell us about it.")

6 Use a questionnaire (see Appendix) to learn more about the student. Revealing questions might include: Who are your favorite TV characters? Who is your favorite relative? What's the funniest thing that ever happened to you? If you could have three wishes, what would they be?

7 Use dramatics in some form. Resist the temptation to always cast the clown in a comedy role. State your faith in his or her competence to handle a straight role. ("Brad, because you seem a natural for the role of the comic, the casting committee has recommended that you take the part of the priest, where you can really demonstrate your acting ability.")

CLUMSINESS

CAPSULE: Clumsy children are as upsetting to themselves as they are to things and people around them.
Dishes and silverware get in their way. Chairs and
tables seem to walk right up to them. They can't play
catch or rollerskate very well. Falling off a horse or a
bike is easy. One doesn't blame them for holding a
healthy disdain for people who seem to glide through
life. They get yelled at for being so clumsy, and often
they strike back in ways that don't increase their popu-
larity. They are students with motor-coordination problems who may elect to compensate for their clumsiness
by spending time doing safe things like reading and sitting around.

According to some literature, one-fifth of elementary-school students have significant motor-skills problems. The family physician may be able to identify the
reasons a child has coordination problems, but the
emphasis should be on helping that student get to
know his or her body and what it can do—with grace.

OPTIONS

1 Arrange for small groups of children with similar problems to work under the direction of the physical education teacher or dance instructor. Note: The physical education teacher can apprise the classroom teacher of the hierarchy of skills the student should attempt.

2 Engage the child in sit-down eye-hand coordination activities, such as marbles or jacks.

3 Give the student gradual experience handling inexpensive breakables. Praise his or her success, no matter how small.

4 Refer the student for a special-education screening. Often the exceptionally clumsy child has a visual-motor learning disability. Through early intervention, the student can learn to deal with and compensate for the disability.

5 Seat the student in an uncongested area, away from breakables.

6 Share your embarrassing moments in class discussion (see Appendix) and mention clumsiness as one of the reasons. ("I'll never forget the time I felt I had two left feet . . . .")

CO-DEPENDENCY

SEE ALSO
Changing Family Structure
Dependency
Stress

CAPSULE: Co-dependency is a compulsion. It is a set of compulsive behaviors learned early in one's life as a means of surviving in a family that is under great emotional strain. Often the family unit includes an alcoholic, critical parents, or a chronically ill person.

Children in such families usually assume roles to help them adjust to the condition prevailing in the home. For instance, a daughter may become a heroine in the role of little mother and counselor. She will work hard to gain praise for managing so well and will enjoy being needed. Another member of the family may find being the scapegoat rewarding in a strange sort of way, so he or she will court trouble on a regular basis. Still another will serve as the family mascot, providing relief as the jester.

Co-dependents have a need to play the part and are attracted to people who need them in some way. Further, they tend to overcommit themselves and try to please others to the exclusion of themselves. In turn, they may become dissatisfied with life, for they never feel that they get back what they give.

OPTIONS

1 Be aware of the student who is blindly loyal to a certain person or an ideal, even when that loyalty is personally harmful.

2 Be aware of the student who tends to judge everything he or she does, says, or thinks by someone else's standards.

3 Be consciously aware of the student who usually seems to value other people's opinions more than his or her own.

4 Consult with the school counselor and social worker who can guide the direction of the student and the family from there on. Family therapy is often advised.

5 Encourage students to keep journals to help them understand themselves, work through some of their problems, and set realistic goals.

SEE ALSO
Attention Seeking
Jealousy
Self-Concept
Tattling

COMPLAINING *CHRONIC*

CAPSULE: The chronic complainer is an unhappy first cousin of the tattler. Things rarely go right for complainers because if they did, complainers would be stripped of their attention-getting device. Chances are complainers imitate someone in the home or neighborhood. In addition to suggestions mentioned in other sections, you might find the following helpful.

OPTIONS

1 Ask complainers to refrain from vocalizing frequently about their unhappiness. Suggest that they submit complaints in writing.

2 Help the students who complain become aware of their attitude by requesting that they state something positive with each complaint. ("Eva, you may not be aware that you are falling into the complaining habit, but the rest of us are. Suppose you allow yourself the luxury of your complaints but always include a plus with your minus, such as 'The cafeteria food tastes bad, but the silverware is clean!' ")

3 Provide an all-school or classroom suggestion box so students can register complaints freely. Deal with the complaints in a democratic manner.

4 Tabulate the student's complaints and present them to him or her. ("Tom, today I recorded the things you complained about. Here they are—twelve of them.") The list could be the basis for a private conference.

COMPULSIVENESS

SEE ALSO
Co-Dependency
Stubbornness

CAPSULE: Compulsive people come in all shapes, colors, and ages. In the classroom, they are the ones who view anything that is loosely organized, free, or spontaneous as a threat. They find comfort in clinging to precision and detail—deviation upsets them. Consumed with detail, this type of person is sometimes labelled rigid, perfectionist, or intolerant. As might be expected, many compulsive children have learned their behavior from a fastidious parent who places order well above divergent thinking. Compulsive students not only fare well but often "overachieve" in highly structured classrooms. There is nothing inherently "wrong" with being compulsive. As with any other quality or behavior, it is the degree that is significant. Watch for opportunities in your classroom to help children experience the harmlessness of trial and error, of taking a chance, or of hazarding a guess.

O P T I O N S

1 Accommodate the compulsive student's need for certainty in one subject and demonstrate the success one can have by trial and error in another. ("Phil, you have learned your rules for decoding well, and this lesson is perfect. Now let's turn to this science problem. Try to find three possible solutions . . . .")

2 Confer with parents to learn to what extent perfection and order are expected at home. Diametrically opposed expectations in the home and in school can confuse a student.

3 Engage the student in activities and assignments that do not put a premium on minute detail and exactness. Discussion and essay questions should focus on open-ended interpretation.

4 Refer the student to the school counselor if compulsiveness seems excessive.

5 Tell the parent you would rather have the child explore more and learn to accept errors than to limit himself or herself for fear of error. (The parent may receive new insight, and the pressures at home may be eased.)

CRUSHES

CAPSULE: Crushes are most common among high-school and college students who are drawn to their teachers for reasons other than scholarship. They also occur on the elementary-school and junior-high levels. The crushes of younger students are usually brief, and, with common sense and courtesy on the part of the teacher, they pass naturally into oblivion.

Symptoms of a "bad case" include a feigned inability to understand a lesson, repeated requests for additional help after school, missing the bus, hanging around, helplessness, and acting out in class—most anything to get attention.

The new teacher, just out of college, is vulnerable. His or her zeal for openness and the desire to be liked are sometimes misinterpreted. Usually, peer pressure keeps the case within bounds in the classroom, but when the mail carrier brings you love notes and you receive telephone calls at your home, you will know you have a problem! There is always the chance that a "spurned" student will make a real or imagined charge against a favorite teacher, so be on your guard!

O P T I O N S

1 Avoid situations that create opportunities to be alone with the smitten student. If a student requires after-school help, make sure that the classroom door is open and other students and/or adults are in view.

2 Have a professional colleague of the same sex as the student talk to him or her if the behavior is excessive or embarrassing.

3 Ignore the student's overtures.

4 Refrain from touching the student. The slightest, most casual touch can be grossly misunderstood.

5 Talk privately with the student. Be aware of the risk involved.

CRYING

SEE ALSO
Stress

C A P S U L E : Crying is a visual expression of emotion and may be interpreted as saying "I feel left out," "I want to punish you," or "I want to be boss." Become an expert in analyzing the differences among types of crying—crying caused by sympathetic feelings for another person or a pet, crying caused by physical hurts or illness, or crying caused by the need for attention or revenge. The latter type is usually the product of a successful tactic both at home and in school. Because tears are among the most powerful of weapons, consistency in dealing with them is absolutely necessary. Parents and teachers should communicate about a united approach to use with the child. Deal warmly and firmly with the student. Remember that any behavior that has become habitual will not be relinquished instantaneously, so be patient (and maybe long-suffering) for the good of the child.

O P T I O N S

1 Ask the student to use the first person when expressing himself or herself. ("I am so angry" instead of "You [he, she] made me do it.") This will check, to some degree, the child's penchant for blaming others and the desire to wallow in self-pity.

2 Consult professional help.

3 Convey the idea that it is the behavior, not the student, that is unsatisfactory. ("I like Sarah, but I get upset when those tears start flowing.")

4 Devise a prevention game with the crier. ("Zach, as soon as you feel a cry coming on, come to my desk and ask for the tissue box. That will be a signal to me that you are feeling upset. It will also be a signal to me to leave you alone until you've dried your tears and we can talk about your feelings.") This places some responsibility on students and tells them you'll be talking later. Keep notes on your talks.

5 Exhibit, without comment, the good work of the child.

6 Interpret for students why they behave in such a way. ("You are bidding for my attention and trying to make me feel guilty when I don't stop everything and give it to you," or "You feel you can't do the work, but you've already shown me you really can, so you must be crying to get my attention.")

7 Listen to what the student says during noncrying moments. Look for clues to feelings about failure, favoritism, or friends. Is he or she modeling the behavior after someone else?

8 Reinforce normal (noncrying) behavior without any reference to the habit of crying. ("Sandy, Jim, and Sue were good sports about being moved to the other team at the last moment. Let's give them a hand.")

9 Hold a staff meeting of all teachers who deal with the crier. Develop strategies to help the student use alternative coping mechanisms. (See Staff Meeting, Appendix.)

CULTURALLY DIVERSE

SEE ALSO
Bilingual Children
Multicultural Population

CAPSULE: For several decades the United States has been defined as the great melting pot in which immigrants are assimilated and the passing of one generation erases many of the stamps of "the old country." That's changing. More and more immigrants are taking on the dual tasks of maintaining their cultural identity and learning to function in American society. All this places a new responsibility on the shoulders of school personnel, for they are expected to help students value their cultures of origin as well as American culture.

OPTIONS

1 Acquaint yourself with sound literature about the cultures of the children from other countries.

2 Demonstrate to your students that you value cultural diversity and express your appreciation in concrete ways. In class, celebrate customs of the varied cultures represented by students.

3 Involve the parents as much as possible when working with their child, but be prepared to find them reticent, at least at first.

4 Work closely with the career counselor to expose minority students to the widest possible range of career opportunities and not just the occupations commonly depicted in films with given ethnic groups.

DANGEROUS CONDUCT

SEE ALSO
Attention Seeking
Bus Conduct
Self-Concept

CAPSULE: The bold, daring students thrive on dangerous conduct. They climb out the classroom window, walk the ledge, and seconds later wave at you from the top of the flagpole. This conduct is a blatant call for attention and help—perhaps an effort to compensate for feelings of inadequacy. Sooner or later they may discover the folly of such conduct, but the price, as well as the fall, may be very shattering. Teachers and parents should caution children to be aware of potentially dangerous situations but also to know the difference between the normal risks of daily living and foolish behavior.

OPTIONS

1 Brainstorm (see Appendix) possibilities of dangerous conduct that could take place around a school. Remember that the brainstorming method of evoking ideas is rapid-fire, and many zany ideas may surface, but they are not to be censored. Exposure of a fascinating, bizarre stunt is not likely to move a student to try it unless he or she already has psychotic tendencies; in fact, the fantasy privilege would, if anything, lessen any desire to try the act.

2 Establish, with the help of the students, safe conduct guidelines.

3 Hold a class discussion that focuses on dangerous conduct in and out of school. The lead question might be: What is the most dangerous thing you ever saw anyone do? Other possibilities are: What's the most dangerous thing you ever did in your life? What compels people to dangerous conduct? What are some ways to discourage others from doing foolish

and dangerous things? (See Class Discussion, Appendix.)

4 Invite a member of the fire department rescue squad to talk about preventing dangerous situations.

5 Take the class on a tour of the school, with the express assignment of detecting zones that might stimulate dangerous conduct. Return to the classroom and discuss your observations.

DAWDLING

SEE ALSO
Wanderers

CAPSULE: Some look upon dawdlers as relaxed, creative thinkers. Perhaps many feel that dawdlers are time wasters who like to deal in trifles. Most will agree that the dawdlers have developed a clever way to forestall detection and scolding because they are physically in motion, doing their "own thing" at a snail's pace. To "Hurry up," they say, "I'm coming." To "Clean your desk," they say, "I'm sorting my crayons." In addition to moving in slow motion, they can figure out the kinds of activities that are just commendable enough to keep you from saying they're not important. After studying the dawdlers through the usual means—past record, health history (How's their hearing?), conferences with those who know the students best—the best approach is to attempt retraining.

OPTIONS

1 Focus on successful attainment of goals within limits. ("David, you should be able to finish your graph in ten minutes," instead of "David, why are you dawdling so when you know you have only fifteen minutes to finish your graph?")

2 Give the dawdler many opportunities to engage in art activities. A study of his or her artwork will give clues to interests, moods, and patterns of behavior. Take care, however, not to read too much into a child's artwork, unless you are professionally trained to do so.

3 Prepare the student for the logical consequences of dawdling (missing an opportunity or activity in the future if the dawdling continues). Having given fair warning, you will not be unjust in leaving the student behind. ("Lindsey, you knew that the bus would leave at 9:40 for the Art Center and you continued to dawdle. Since you are not ready and the bus must leave, I've made arrangements for you to work in Miss Bennett's room until we return.") Reaping the consequences of his or her conduct may sharpen the student's awareness of the problem.

4 Refer the child for a special-education screening. He or she may have a learning disability, processing problem, or visual/hearing problem.

5 Talk to the dawdler about this pattern of behavior and listen to his or her ideas about the conduct. (Is the student bored? Tired? Hungry? Lonely?)

6 Use videotaping to show students how to behave. Seeing yourself as others see you can be a powerful motivator for change!

DAYDREAMING

SEE ALSO

Attention Deficit Disorder
Attention Span
Withdrawn Children

CAPSULE: Daydreaming is a pleasant form of escape. Reverie, being lost in thought, is as harmless as any form of inattention, but it can be annoying to a teacher when attentiveness is crucial to learning. Adolescent students are often physically present but are not really paying attention because their minds are wandering. When called upon, they may act as though they are hard of hearing. Although some daydreaming is normal, the following suggestions may enhance attention.

OPTIONS

1 Allow some daydreaming. Make an issue over chronic patterns only.

2 Refer the student for a special-education screening if a chronic pattern persists and inattentiveness seriously affects learning. What appears to be excessive daydreaming may be a symptom of Attention Deficit Disorder or other condition.

3 Vary activities during a lesson to involve students. Make sure that students have many opportunities for active participation. Students may be prone to daydreaming when they feel they are listening to an interminable lecture by a "sage on the stage."

DEALING WITH DEATH

SEE ALSO
Suicide

CAPSULE: The death of a loved one or even an acquaintance is a traumatic experience for all people. Children are not excluded from the emotions surrounding the loss of a family member or friend. The death of a sibling, parent, or classmate can have short- and long-term effects on a student's performance in and out of school. Common response behaviors are bedwetting, nail biting, nightmares, stealing, failure in school work, and bizarre, impulsive actions.

According to some studies of mental hospital admissions, the death of a parent may contribute to mental illness, depression, and attempted suicide. The suppression of grief may signal problems ahead. Many students will experience a delayed reaction to the loss and will exhibit unusual behaviors weeks or months after the death. Bereaved students need to be able to release their feelings in a safe place, with trusted individuals such as teachers or counselors.

O P T I O N S

1 Become conversant with the now well-established phases of grief (denial, anger, bargaining, depression, acceptance). Understanding the process will enable you to accept the child's response to life in and out of school. Be open and honest with the student. Encourage the student to express his or her feelings.

2 Communicate the fact that you too feel the loss, if you do, and that showing emotions is normal. Tears are a sincere tribute to the person who has died. You may want to share your personal views of death, if the child asks. Go easy on euphemisms.

3 Establish a school protocol, perhaps a "crisis intervention" plan, to help the bereaved student and other children in the school to deal with loss. If no crisis intervention plan is in place, look to other schools for appropriate models.

4 Make sure that all school personnel are aware of the death and the surrounding circumstances so that they can communicate sensitively and appropriately to the bereaved child.

5 Refrain from giving the child pat answers and/or trite responses to deep pain, such as "You're working too hard," or "You're not getting enough rest." That kind of talk only pushes the subject aside.

6 Use bibliotherapy (see Appendix). Alcott's *Little Women* is a classic example of a book that helps children come to terms with grief.

DEMONSTRATIVENESS

SEE ALSO
Crushes

CAPSULE: Students smitten with "puppy love" or deeper feelings often manifest their affection with little inhibition on the campus, on the bus, in the hallways, and in the classroom. Any reminder, no matter how tactful, might be met with disdain. Often, insecure youth latch onto a "steady" and feel obliged to convey the "hands off" message by being ultrademonstrative. When the romance is over, you can expect at least one of the parties to feel "dumped," making "never again" pronouncements. What should one do when "PDA" (public displays of affection) actually interferes with the student's learning and with effective instruction? Sometimes demonstrative behavior goes beyond hand-holding and "making out" to overt sexual groping. Approach the matter with sensitivity, openness, and excellent teaching, which are deterrents, if not cures.

OPTIONS

1 Discuss acceptable social and sexual conduct in class or in small groups. With the ever-increasing AIDS epidemic, as well as the increase in other sexually transmitted diseases, no time is too soon to discuss responsible sexual behavior. Demonstrative behavior can be a springboard for teacher-led discussions on abstinence as the only form of safe sex and other forms of "safer" sex.

2 Hold an Ann Landers meeting (see Appendix). The first questioner might say, "I'd like to know what some of you think about showing affection for each other in school." Count on conservative as well as "boundless" points of view to surface.

3 Show the students that your heart isn't cold by good-naturedly referring to their demonstrative behavior. ("Jan and Don, you're going to need all four hands for this next assignment, so why don't you move your desks apart and grab on to this string that's being passed around?")

4 Take aside overly demonstrative students and discuss appropriate public behavior. Explain that classrooms, hallways, and courtyards are not places for intimate expressions of affection.

DEPENDENCY

SEE ALSO
Co-Dependency
Self-Concept

CAPSULE: Dependent children hesitate to act before they have the teacher's approval. They may have been conditioned to behave this way by overprotective or critical parents. Somehow, they have come to feel that they can't trust themselves and must depend on others. It is not uncommon for overly dependent children to resist learning to read. While this kind of behavior is most evident from ages four to six, it can persist into adulthood. Eventually, such people may come to hate those who fostered their dependence, because they were robbed of precious times during which they should have been thinking for themselves.

OPTIONS

1 Confer with the parents and agree upon strategies that will develop the child's independence. If it becomes clear that the parents handle the child inconsistently, perhaps you should refer them to the school counselor or psychologist.

2 Encourage the student to identify something that is troubling. Through brainstorming, help the student discover ways to cope with the problem. He or she may begin by (1) naming the problem, (2) determining the cause of the problem, (3) predicting the solution that might succeed, and (4) trying out the favored hypothesis. *Note:* This approach may be used at any age level.

3 Praise obvious efforts to become more independent. ("I was glad to see you walk home from school by yourself today, Gina.")

4 Seat the child by an independent worker who will not "help" the child but will provide a good model.

5 Show the student how to use what he or she has learned. ("Bill, you have learned your multiplication tables; now use them to solve this problem.")

6 Wean the child away from dependency by establishing a hierarchy of steps and moving him or her through it (see School Phobia).

DEPRESSION

SEE ALSO
Discouraged Children
Fearfulness
Self-Concept
Suicide
Underachievers

CAPSULE: *Webster's* defines depression as "an emotional condition characterized by sadness, inactivity, and a feeling of inadequacy." Everyone from time to time experiences depression in small doses. Often referred to as "feeling down," when the blues won't go away, depression has likely set in. Long-lasting depression is an illness that requires attention.

Like adults, children are susceptible to bouts of depression. The depressed student may wear a mantle of hopelessness reflected in a sloppy manner of dressing, withdrawal from society, difficulty in handling strong feelings, and frequent irritability. Depressed children may also exhibit behaviors ranging from sleeping too much to inability to sleep, as well as changes in clothing, eating, social, and work habits. An attitude of gloom and doom may prevail, as depressed children withdraw from family, friends, and school.

Depression may have a number of causes. Primary depression is caused by a chemical imbalance and can be treated medically. Other forms of depression can be treated through psychotherapy or counseling. Only a specialist can diagnose and determine treatment for depression.

OPTIONS

1 Be alert to the signs of depression. Contact the family. Sometimes family therapy is recommended.

2 Consider the use of bibliotherapy (see Appendix). The school librarian may be able to provide books with plots focusing on certain concerns of youth.

3 Discuss the student at a staff meeting (see Appendix). The school nurse, psychologist, and social worker should be present to help give direction.

4 Recommend to parents that they refer the student to a physician. The doctor will be able to determine if the depression has a medical cause such as anemia or a chemical imbalance. If and when medical causes are ruled out, the physician may refer the student for alternative treatment, such as some form of counseling.

5 Remind yourself that everyone gets depressed at times. Only abnormal students would not feel "down" if they were not experiencing success at school or if they had experienced a loss.

6 Venture to talk with the student on a one-to-one basis, and show your interest and concern. ("I've noticed a certain quietness about you lately, Joe. Maybe it isn't any of my business, but you seem pretty somber. Are you okay? Just wanted you to know I care.")

SEE ALSO
Cheating
Lying

DEVIOUSNESS

CAPSULE: Deviousness implies manipulation and deception. Devious students have lost trust in adults. They feel that they can deal with adults best through trickery. Adults working with devious students have the task of convincing them that they can achieve their goals through more direct routes.

Devious individuals often pit one person against another in order to get their way. Sometimes students choose to play one teacher against another. Allowed to go on, the situation will likely fester. Early, straightforward resolution is recommended.

OPTIONS

1 Be generous in your praise of the student who is habitually devious but who surprisingly breaks the pattern. The student may catch the message that directness carries its reward. ("You gave a very direct answer to Mr. Z. when he questioned you about _____, and it was easy to see that he admired you for it.")

2 Refuse to submit to the devious student's effort to trap you into open rejection of his or her behavior. ("Let's try that again, Rick. This time, let's communicate honestly and openly.")

3 Show the student you prefer straightforwardness instead of beating around the bush. ("Give it to me straight now, Sandy. Save the detours for another time.")

4 Trust the student. If you cannot, tell the student why you are skeptical and demonstrate that you are ready to help him or her cope with problems honestly. Your sincere concern will break down some of his or her defenses.

SEE ALSO
Disabilities, Learning
Disabilities, Physical

DISABILITIES *DEVELOPMENTAL*

CAPSULE: A developmental disability is a condition that interferes with the normal development of an individual, resulting in a need for assistance in daily activities, such as movement, communication, and self-care, to encourage optimum independence. Mental retardation is the most common developmental disability. It is a condition of subnormal intellectual and social development. While the learning disabled child has a specific deficiency, the mentally challenged child has an overall deficiency.

OPTIONS

1 Be mindful that the education of the child should focus on skills that will help him or her become increasingly independent.

2 Create a situation in which the mentally challenged student will be socially accepted. If your classroom is "the least restrictive environment," incorporate cooperative learning (see Appendix) and other group activities. In properly structured groups, the disabled student should find a way to contribute academically and participate socially.

3 Encourage the disabled student to participate actively in the class. Vary the level of questioning (according to Bloom's Taxonomy—see Appendix) and make sure that you give the disabled student enough time to process answers.

4 Use some of your more able students to help the student with drill and routine activities.

5 Visit with the parents, social worker, and counselor periodically about the child's progress.

DISABILITIES *LEARNING*

SEE ALSO
Nutritional Deficiencies
Reading Problems
Self-Concept

CAPSULE: Learning disabilities are disorders that impede a child's ability to learn. Children with learning disabilities may seem normal in every way to the casual observer, but may find processing information difficult. Consequently, students with learning disabilities often do poorly in school.

The range of difficulties manifested is wide. One student may have trouble speaking, another concentrating, another remembering or memorizing. For instance, children with perception disorders suffer when trying to read. They may not be able to distinguish between words that are similar or they may not be able to tell where one word ends and another begins. Some learning disabilities interfere with the child's muscle control. Others damage a child's sense of space and direction.

The causes of a child's particular disability are elusive, but evidence points to brain damage as one of them. Poor nutrition and the mother's use of hard drugs or alcohol during pregnancy are more than suspect. Also, medical research has discovered that certain chemicals, such as lead, may trigger learning disabilities.

Because children with learning disabilities feel they have little control over their environment, they are often disruptive in school.

O P T I O N S

1 Confer with the parents. Learn from them how they perceive the child's learning situation.

2 Observe closely and document symptoms of learning disabilities.

3 Refer the child to specialists for diagnosis. A thorough screening will include examinations by a pediatrician, eye and ear specialist, a special education teacher, and a psychologist. Treat the child according to professional recommendations.

4 Refrain from labeling students who are disruptive or are experiencing learning problems as learning disabled. Not all behavioral or learning problems can be categorized as disabilities.

DISABILITIES *PHYSICAL*

SEE ALSO
Eye Problems
Hearing Problems

C A P S U L E : The child with physical disabilities deserves special attention, for every person with physical challenges is unique. Under federal law (Public Law 94-142), schools are now required to enable such children to get an education "in the least restrictive environment." Mainstreaming is now general policy and requires the utmost cooperation by family and faculty. The attitude of the community and faculty makes all the difference.

The law further requires a multidisciplinary team to conduct a comprehensive evaluation of each disabled child's educationally relevant strengths and weaknesses. Based on these data, the counseling staff, teachers, and other specialists develop an Individualized Educational

Plan (IEP) designed to meet each student's needs. Modes of complying with the legal requirements vary from school to school, but the least restrictive mandate applies in all cases.

OPTIONS

1 Acquaint yourself with local and state services for assisting children with disabilities if family resources are limited. The Kiwanis, Rotary, and Lions clubs are noted for their generosity and civic-mindedness.

2 Consult a physican for recommendations on educational placement. The school counselor or social worker may also provide recommendations and advice.

3 Discuss the progress of the child in regular staff meetings (see Appendix).

4 Help a physically challenged student develop a matter-of-fact attitude toward his or her disability. By your own attitude, help classmates develop a wholesome, whole-person response to the student as a person. Able-bodied students are interested in knowing about the student with disabilities. Find ways for the children to exchange information, ask questions, and learn about one another in an open, friendly manner. Deal with sneers or hurtful ridicule with dispatch.

5 Record and fix in your mind critical issues regarding the safety of the student. Pay strict attention to emergency measures.

6 Show sensitivity to family members of the disabled student, who may also have special problems related to acceptance of the child and their own positions in the family.

7 Work closely with the parents of the child so that the adjustment of all the students, able-bodied and disabled, goes as smoothly as possible.

DISCOURAGED CHILDREN

SEE ALSO
Fearfulness
Self-Concept
Underachievers

CAPSULE: Discouraged children must be helped to conquer the fears that dominate their behavior. They may cower in a cloak of average or respectable performance rather than endeavor to excel, because they are afraid of failing, afraid of appearing silly or stupid, afraid of being made fun of by people who rate high with them, afraid of calling attention to themselves—afraid, afraid, afraid. The renowned bacteriologist August von Wasserman, we are told, failed over six hundred times before he succeeded in producing the serum that bears his name. What a pity if he had stopped just one try short of success! Teachers must become experts at helping students accept errors as part of problem solving instead of as stigmatic seals of disapproval. When errors become stepping stones instead of ledges on which to perch unhappily, they may be more effective than a series of rapid-fire successes.

Students need to have acknowledgment of their efforts and to distinguish between short- and long-range goals. Occasionally, the long-range goals set forth by adults in their lives are so far-reaching and frightening that they can't even do anything about the immediate goals. Student involvement in establishing objectives diminishes this kind of stress; it also makes teaching easier and more fun.

The discouraged student also needs to be shown how an idea can transform inactivity into power. Never underestimate the power of an idea; it is potency personified. Its place is in the classroom. Students need recognition for their efforts. Definitive rejection kills; a spark of recognition kindles.

Discouraged students become hopeful through (1) recognition of their honest efforts, (2) a vision of attainable goals, (3) elimination of fear of failure, and (4) a promise of experiencing something that has special significance or value to them. You may add ideas of your own to the following, which may be used with the discouraged student.

OPTIONS

1 Acknowledge the student's contributions without put-downs, sarcasm, or half-hearted acceptance. ("That's an idea, Lindy!")

2 Ask a discouraged child to teach others how to do something. ("Grant, Shawn would like to you to teach him how to tie his shoelaces," or "Marnie, you are the only one in the class who knows anything about Japanese paper folding; could you teach these boys who want to learn to make folded fish?")

3 Display samples of the student's work that will call others' attention to his or her capabilities. Peer motivation is potent.

4 Enlist the discouraged student's help in tutoring younger children, and hold the student responsible for recommending techniques that will work. Some of the discouraged one's ideas may then be turned into useful ways of working with him or her.

5 Help the student analyze possible reasons for the state of discouragement through leading questions such as, "Who are you most like, your mother or your father?" "What subject holds your interest the longest and why?" "If money were no object, what would you like to do for a living?"

6 Individualize and personalize some of the student's assignments and assignment schedule. The graduated progression built into the lessons should be encouraging. (See Flight Plan, Appendix)

7 Talk to the student, in an informal setting outside the classroom, about his or her hopes and aspirations. Restate some of them so that the student knows that you understand and can help clarify his or her thinking. ("Justin, you like playing your sax and drums more than anything else in the world. Making a living playing in a band is your big dream.")

DOMINEERING CHILDREN

SEE ALSO
Abrasiveness
Bullying

CAPSULE: Domineering describes people who behave arbitrarily and overbearingly and who want to be boss. Whatever the explainable reasons for this attitude, they are usually unpopular. Perhaps physical size, place in the family, or model of conduct (domineering father or mother) contribute significantly to the attitude of domineering children. Very often they are aggressive on the athletic field and, at the same time, poor losers because their familes have placed unrealistic emphasis on winning or on upholding a family record. Whatever accounts for their loud, dogmatic approach to dealing with others, they should reduce the intensity of conduct in order to get along well with others inside and outside of the classroom.

OPTIONS

1 Counsel the domineering student. ("Michael, you create some problems for yourself with your domineering attitude.") Suggest then that the student may be dominating situations because he or she wants to be the "big shot," wants to "put some people in their place and even a score," or simply craves attention and doesn't know how else to get it. When the student is able to state his or her goal, you will be in a position to help the student attack the problem. However, the initiative for behavioral change must come from the student.

2 Establish time limits for talking or using materials. "Deborah, your time is up. Now it's Johanna's turn."

3 Reinforce any small sign of improved behavior. ("Jenny, you are working like a good team member.")

4 Solicit from your students, through class discussions, ways of coping with abrasive behaviors, which could include a domineering attitude, and agree to try some of the approaches if incidents ever arise. For example, the class may decide that a domineering student will be asked by the class chairperson to leave the room until he or she can be a contributing member of the group. Peer pressure is often more effective than adult pressure.

5 Videotape small-group activities that may reveal very clearly that the domineering student is inclined to take over. Discuss the film objectively, asking each student to evaluate his or her own behavior, not that of others. Expect observations such as "I didn't realize that I talked so much!" or "I didn't realize I'm so quiet."

DRESS PROBLEMS

CAPSULE: Although fashions constantly change and schools may adjust rules according to fashion dictates, most schools have guidelines based on a guiding principle: a student's choice of clothing should not interfere with the learning of others. Teachers and school officials have to decide whether shirts with suggestive slogans or cut-out (not "cut-off") jeans present learning distractions. Dress codes, which were once standard procedure in most schools, are dwindling in public schools and are being challenged in some private schools. In most private and military schools, dress problems do not exist.

School authorities should remember that unless they have planned cooperatively with the students, parents, and faculty on how to deal with the dress and grooming problem, they may have trouble. Further, if the same authorities cannot be happy without dictating the code, they had better look for a safe retreat. Rigid regulations regarding dress and grooming bespeak a single-value system and nullify lofty claims to "recognition of individual differences." This is not to say that controls regarding school dress are completely passé; it is rather a plea for emphasis on standards of conduct, not school rules. This approach minimizes friction over proper school dress.

Pertinent reminders: If a dress code exists, it should be widely publicized through school news media (handbook, newspaper, daily bulletins). Parents should be apprised of the dress code by means of an official communication. When dress matters are discussed with an offender, the adult who has the best rapport with the student should handle the issue in a non-confrontational manner. Furthermore, a student's attire shouldn't affect his or her grades one way or the other. A rule of thumb might be: Fads come and go. Don't let them throw you. If the fads don't interfere with learning, don't do anything unless you're sure that you're the best judge or that you must be in control to that extent.

Beyond fads, which are usually affordable for they may be no more consequential than wearing unmatched socks or a single earring, pressure exists among youth to wear more expensive "designer" clothes. Not only are the students nudged into *wanting* designer fashions, but the parents are faced with either resisting the pressure or giving in. Peer pressure, snobbishness, and fear of rejection are some of the forces that lead to clothing competition. Although the family must reckon with the problem, teachers can help students define and understand their values.

OPTIONS

1 Apprise students of areas in which rules are firm, and at the same time remind them of areas in which they may establish their own rules and of how to go about doing so.

2 Be firm, but kind, when it becomes necessary to withdraw a student from class (or school) because of indecent apparel. Use "I" messages in talking with the student. ("Ginny, I need to tell you that I'm uncomfortable with the length of your skirt. I'd like to ask you to change clothes and not to wear that skirt to school again.")

3 Compliment the student in question when he or she is pleasingly attired, but be matter-of-fact. ("That's a pretty outfit, Elizabeth," instead of "Wow!")

4 Discuss the psychology of fashion—how everything we do tells something about our inner drives and motivation. This kind of discussion is a natural in social studies, literature, and psychology classes.

5 Enforce consistently any rules of dress, good speech, and so forth that have been adopted.

6 Enlist parents' aid in determining appropriate clothing for school and in helping students to come to school wearing mutually agreed-upon attire.

7 Review the dress code with the student whose dress is in question and jointly conclude whether an infringement has occurred. Then consider alternatives.

DRINKING

SEE ALSO
Drug Use
Health Problems

CAPSULE: In many schools, alcohol has become the drug of choice. Because of liquor's easy availability in stores and within students' homes, to many the word "party" has become synonymous with drinking. Schools can attack the problem by establishing and enforcing stringent no-alcohol guidelines for participation in school-sponsored events. The entire school community must be educated about the extent of student drinking and its effects.

OPTIONS

1 Confront the student privately and point out that alcohol has no place in the school setting. Then listen to him or her for clues that will tell you something of the degree of the problem. Does the student bring a flask to classes? Where does he get the money for alcoholic beverages? Does liquor flow freely in the family? Is the family fanatically anti-drinking? Is the student having academic, romantic, or economic problems? Find out whether the drinking incident is a one-shot deal or a confirmed pattern. If in doubt, go easy and be sure to let the student know you are a friend.

2 Consult school health personnel. Recommend a staff meeting (see Appendix) be held to discuss the student.

3 Demonstrate and uphold the idea that every act carries its own consequences. ("Sam, you know alcohol has no place in our basketball training program, and our code of conduct states pretty clearly that you are now out of Saturday's game. I'm sorry, because we need your speed and accuracy against Monmouth, but that's the way it is, and I doubt that it will happen again.")

4 Encourage students to make studies of problems stemming from drinking through

data available from local agencies, news media, and professional people. Give them the privilege of choosing speakers and inviting them to class.

5 Establish a SADD (Students Against Drunk Driving) chapter in the school. Students and teachers working together can enlighten others about problems (and tragedies) caused by drinking. The group can also work toward preventing such tragedies within the school community.

6 Implement a schoolwide procedure for dealing with students who come to class with symptoms of alcohol abuse. For example, if a student smells of alcohol, the teacher might send him or her to the nurse or other school authority. If drinking is confirmed, parents should be notified so that together, school and home can develop strategies to resolve the problem.

7 Make films, filmstrips, and videotapes available for viewing in a club setting free of a "tight and teachy" atmosphere. Also, library carrels or resource centers provide excellent places for students to view films or listen to tapes privately.

8 Start a substance-abuse-prevention program within the school. In homeroom, in health class, and in units in other classes, educate students about the dangers of alcohol and other drugs. In the school district, hire a student assistance coordinator to work with the faculty on how to detect signs of drinking. The coordinator can also work with students and parents on how to prevent and treat drinking problems.

9 Suspend drinking students from school for a limited time and re-admit them when parents or guardians accompany them to school. Suspension is handled by the administrators, not the teachers. *Caution:* The longer the students are out of school, the farther behind they will get in work. Suspension doesn't treat the cause of the behavior, only the symptom. However, suspension compels students to reflect on the problem, and parents become involved. This fact can bring latent and not-so-latent emotions to the fore, calling for experienced, skillful counseling.

DROPOUTS *POTENTIAL*

SEE ALSO
Loneliness
Self-Concept
Underachievers

CAPSULE: Students drop out of school for many reasons, including academic failure, social stress, and environmental pressure. The elementary teacher would do well to remember that at this very moment through grouping and other practices, he or she may inadvertently be preparing a future dropout. Frequent analyses of dropouts reflect the beginnings of failure in the elementary grades. Dropouts are usually lonely, disillusioned people. Ask yourself whether your smiles and nods of acceptance have contributed to students hanging in there as long as they have or whether your scowls and judgmental attitudes have pushed them out! If you're serious about helping a potential dropout, you will most likely have to work on self-esteem and empowerment issues.

O P T I O N S

1 Arouse the student's ambition to realize an attainable goal. Capitalize on a talent he or she has, such as singing or assembling motors, and enable the student to use this skill in meeting a specific assignment in a class. ("Today during science we'll all go to the local garage and Phil will demonstrate how to take a motor apart.") Accent the student's strengths and encourage him or her to build on successes.

2 Consider a flexible work-study schedule for the student, if financial distress might lead to the student's dropping out of school. ("Lauren, if you can arrange to work for Mr. J. at the filling station every Thursday morning, we can adjust your class schedule.")

3 Create a warm climate in the classroom where diversity is welcomed and individual strengths are rewarded. Inform the troubled student that, with effort, he or she can and will succeed. When assigning grades, reward effort and achievement.

4 Hold a staff meeting (see Appendix) to garner all possible pertinent information, and select the most competent and empathetic person to follow through with the team's recommendations.

5 Identify potential dropouts and work with the parents, fellow teachers, and administrators in developing effective strategies, policies, and interventions, some of which are mentioned above.

6 Recognize the student's goals as he or she talks to you, and restate them. ("What you seem to be saying is that none of your course work will ever help you be what you want to be. Let's consider some alternatives in your case.")

7 Welcome a former dropout back to school with open arms. Enabling students to finish school may diminish the cost to society of unemployment and crime. The educational reform movement advocating excellence in the schools begins with an ounce of prevention—salvaging the potential dropout.

DRUG USE

SEE ALSO
Drinking
Loneliness
Self-Concept
Underachievers

C A P S U L E : The problem of drug abuse straddles all types of students in all socioeconomic classes. Approximately 20 percent of all middle and high-school students experience drug use or abuse. Generally, 8 to 12 percent of students require treatment for drug abuse before they graduate high school.

Students often succumb to their first experience because of peer pressure: "Just try a hit." School authorities need to be on the constant lookout for pushers, sometimes members of gangs, who infiltrate the school. Parents and teachers should (1) acquaint themselves with the vocabulary or slang terms used in the drug culture, (2) observe the friendships developing—rarely will a user trust a nonuser enough to associate with him or her, and (3) be aware of dramatic changes in attitude, attendance, scholarship, personality, dress, friends, best friend, and sports and activities participation.

New drugs hit the streets periodically. In the last decade *crack* has become extremely prevalent. A lethal form of cocaine, it is sometimes called *free base* because when it is refined from cocaine hydrochloride, it is freed from its base. Crack's effects reach the brain in six seconds, producing euphoria. The user is immediately intoxicated and feels invincible, but the "dropoff" is so unpleasant that he or she will do most anything for another "hit." The desire for more induces the child to steal, lie, and fight to get cash for more.

Teachers report that the primary grades are now enrolling children whose mothers were crack users. Learning disabilities can sometimes be traced to a mother's use of drugs.

School boards and administrative staff are required to report any suspicion of drugs or alcohol and will be deemed negligent if they fail to report drug abuse to the prescribed chain of authority. Many schools are also adding Student Assistant Program coordinators to their staffs to provide information and implement prevention and intervention techniques.

OPTIONS

1 Arrange a continuous drug education program starting in the early elementary grades. Primary and middle schools may want to get involved with the "Just Say No" program. Middle and secondary schools may want to initiate antidrug programs in which esteem and trust are built among peers and between students and adults. The Department of Education, Washington, D.C., can provide information on package programs.

2 Consider the possibility of holding drug education meetings away from the school building to enhance a total community response to the drug problem.

3 Encourage students to conduct and share simple, scientific research studies on the subject of drugs.

4 Engage students in extracurricular activities. Busy, productive, happy students are less likely to be susceptible to negative peer pressure that can lead to drug abuse.

5 Get to know students on an informal basis. Frequent the halls, gyms, and playgrounds. Discern, if you can, possible reasons why certain students turn to drugs (family, grades, friends, unpopularity, health, fears, and so on).

6 Institute a program for recovering users. Especially if students have received

medical treatment or have been hospitalized, they will need a transitional, supportive program to help make the adjustment to the school routine. Meeting in small groups to discuss common problems, under the direction of a counselor, can be helpful.

7 Look for evidence of dysfunctional family life (see Co-Dependency, Appendix). In families where recreational drugs are used, students often take on "locked-in roles," such as the hero, scapegoat, or mascot.

8 Provide meaningful outlets that carry responsibility and might supplant the need for drugs (theater, sports, or art, for example).

9 Recognize the student who is under the influence of drugs. Mood swings are

common. Other clues include: red and watery eyes (glue); red, raw nostrils (cocaine); profuse perspiration and body odor, constant licking of lips to keep them moist, and tremor of hands (amphetamines); runny nose (heroin, morphine, codeine); long-sleeved garments to hide needle tracks (heroin, Methedrine); sunglasses worn at inappropriate times to hide dilated pupils (LSD); and staggering and disorientation (barbiturates). Remember that many of these symptoms also identify other ailments.

10 Refer an identified drug user to a counselor, medical personnel, or Student Assistance Program coordinator, all with the utmost discretion. Ex-users may also provide useful advice.

EATING DISORDERS

SEE ALSO
Anxiety
Eating Problems
Health Problems

CAPSULE: Thousands of adolescent girls and young women, and to a lesser extent boys and young men, are afflicted every year by eating disorders. The two most common disorders are *anorexia nervosa* and *bulimia nervosa.*

Anorexics choose to starve themselves, sometimes to an emaciated state, because they want to be thin. Bulimics opt to binge, then purge, so as not to get fat. Both are victims of their perceived notion that they will have more worth if they are slender. They both suffer psychological problems, and in order to resolve their conflicts, the family must become involved.

Typically, anorexics and bulimics come from families whose members are very dependent upon each other and who find it hard to handle their anger and stress. "Intertwined" describes such a family. Often anorexic people feel out of control, and the one area they *can* control is what (and how) they eat.

Indicators of a potential eating disorder are a marked change in eating behavior and loss of weight, changes in social conduct, such as giving excuses for not eating with the family or the peer group, over-enthusiasm for exercising, an obsession with getting on the scales, and frequent trips to the bathroom. There are also changes in the person's psychosocial behavior, including much talk about size and a need to diet.

O P T I O N S

1 Arrange for peer counseling or a recovered anorexic or bulimic to work with the student.

2 Become knowledgeable about co-dependency so that you can better understand the student (see Appendix).

3 Encourage the family to seek counseling. Contact support groups in the community and be ready to relay the information when it is appropriate. The family physician will have this information. A physician and a nutritionist can help the student solve the problem.

4 Pay attention to students who appear to be losing a great amount of weight or who are constantly talking about dieting.

5 Tell parents or the student that they may write to American Anorexia/Bulimia Association, Dept. P, 133 Cedar Lane, Teaneck, NJ 07666, for current information on the disorders. Other addresses may be obtained from the local support group in your area.

EATING PROBLEMS

SEE ALSO
Anxiety
Eating Disorders
Health Problems

CAPSULE: Students who don't eat well or who regularly gag or vomit during lunchtime are emitting a message to be interpreted. Most likely, these children are so fear-ridden that their bodies are not able to handle input. Finicky eaters may have emotional problems.

Students react to the climate of the lunchroom. Stand back for a moment and watch the crowded cafeteria lines, the quantities of "fillers" shoved at the students, the time limits on eating, the rules, the policing, the din or the quiet, the exclusiveness, the drabness, and the sameness. For many students, lunchtime, instead of providing a respite from school pressures, creates additional pressure.

OPTIONS

1 Ask the student which person he or she would like to sit by while eating, and discreetly arrange it.

2 Confer with the parents, the school nurse, or a physician.

3 Consult the child's school record for clues.

4 Elicit from the student, privately, any mealtime worries. Be nondirective. ("To you, lunchtime isn't a very fun time of the day.") If you make the mistake of asking a question, you will have to be satisfied with a "yes" or "no," period!

5 Give the child some options regarding the food. ("Max, will you have half an apple or a whole one?") This not only gives the child an opportunity to make a choice, but places some responsibility on him or her.

6 Have an older student eat with the child.

7 Present a hypothetical or real case for class discussion (see Appendix). One example: "I once knew a student who got very upset during lunchtime in school. Sometimes he even gagged and threw up. It took us a long time to find out why. What do you think might have been the matter?"

8 Provide enjoyable activities for students to participate in immediately after lunch. Recess or playing games in the gym may help to relax students who feel tense during lunch.

ECCENTRICITY

CAPSULE: Eccentric students are different from the rest. They may be whimsically so because of a penchant for a unique wardrobe, or they may be different enough to suggest mild mental aberration. They may be very lonely or they may be the happiest ones in the lot.

Very often, eccentric children are pressured by adults to be more "well rounded and typical," which they clearly do not prefer. Respect eccentric children for their individuality. Their ideas may be offbeat, but their very eccentricity may spawn great revolutionary ideas!

Children, being what they are, can be both charitable and cruel. It requires the sensitivity of a concertmaster to deflect unkind comments regarding eccentricity. Your attitude of general acceptance will provide the best model for your students.

O P T I O N S

1 In a class discussion (see Appendix), encourage your students to recognize and appreciate the uniqueness of people. Use literary models as well as real people. ("In what ways are Justin and Adam *alike?* In what ways are they *different?* In what ways are they *unusual?*")

2 Get acquainted with the eccentric child's family, so that you can better understand him or her. This should be done with any child, but it may be particularly necessary in the case of the student with eccentricities.

3 Give the eccentric child a special task that nobody else could (or would) do quite as well: photographer for the yearbook, for instance, or statistician for the football team.

4 Help the eccentric student pursue his or her studies through individualized, personalized lessons. (See Flight Plan, Appendix.)

5 Recognize a product, a special talent, or a deed of the eccentric one. For example, buy one of his or her artworks that may be in an exhibit, ask for a copy of a poem he or she wrote, or write the student a note of appreciation for a deed.

6 Show the eccentric student, in inconspicuous ways, that he or she is important to you. A smile, a nod, a touch, a request to do an errand, or a listening ear will all be effective.

EPILEPSY

SEE ALSO
Health Problems

CAPSULE: Epilepsy is a physical impairment that is often misunderstood. Too often a child with normal or above intelligence is misdiagnosed as retarded because of epilepsy. More than four million people in the U.S. have some form of epilepsy; the most common types are referred to as *grand mal* and *petit mal.*

Epilepsy is a disorder marked by disturbed electrical rhythms of the central nervous system. Anticonvulsant medication is used to control the seizures, which can occur without warning. School personnel should be knowledgeable about the disorder and should be prepared to respond effectively if a student has an attack in school.

A *grand mal* seizure involves unconsciousness, falling to the ground, frothing at the mouth, involuntary jerking of the limbs, and eyes rolling upward. During a *petit mal* attack, the victim loses awareness of his or her surroundings for only a few seconds. Some epileptics have psychomotor attacks during which they act withdrawn and behave strangely for a few minutes. They may suddenly take off and wander around the room for a few minutes or begin yanking at their clothes in a strange, repetitive manner.

O P T I O N S

1 Acquaint yourself with proper procedure in case a student has a seizure. Try to situate the person in an open area. Be sure there are no sharp objects around. Loosen any tight clothing, such as belts, ties, or scarves. Refrain from placing an object in the person's mouth to prevent tongue biting unless you know how to place the project properly.

2 Ask medical personnel in the community to conduct an inservice training program for the faculty on developmental disabilities and associated medical disorders.

3 Be sure to alert any substitute teachers to an epileptic student in the class.

4 Handle the loss of bladder or bowel control judiciously.

5 Institute a support group of students who have chronic health problems.

6 Keep calm. Refrain from becoming hysterical or exciting the other students. Once the incident has subsided, use the happening to help the students' understanding of epilepsy. Providing straightforward factual information is the best procedure.

7 Send another student for the nurse immediately. Notify the parents of the seizure.

EXHIBITIONISM

SEE ALSO
Obscenities
Self-Concept

CAPSULE: Exhibitionism is not one of the most common problems encountered in schools, but it does occur. When the high-school senior flexes his muscles and his friends call him an "exhibitionist," they are, of course, being facetious. If he were an exhibitionist, his behavior would be of an obscene, psychosexual nature.

News of the exhibitionist usually gets around—in whispers. To be sure, cases of obscene conduct should be reported to the proper person, but they should be factual, firsthand reports. On-the-spot reprimanding and embarrassment will add nothing to the correction of the behavior.

Little children's early explorations of the world—of which their own bodies are a part—may include masturbation and childhood exhibitionism of the "I'll-show-you-if-you-show-me" variety, which scarcely qualifies for the traditional "show and tell" agenda. At any rate, numerous studies show that this kind of behavior diminishes around age five.

The classroom is the least likely place for exhibition, but there are other protected areas around a school where crowds cluster and supervision is minimal. Should you be confronted with this kind of a problem, keep your cool and rely on your relationship with the student to handle the matter with dignity.

O P T I O N S

1 Be sensitive to other students' reactions to the exhibitionist, but don't make the subject a conversation matter.

2 Mention the incident to the parents. They need to know in case exhibitionism becomes a repeated pattern.

3 Speak to someone you can trust about the incident and refer the problem to professionals trained to deal with such behavior.

4 Talk to the student privately sometime after the incident, at a time when other students are not aware of the conference. Expect his or her greatest fear to be your reporting the exhibitionism. Explain that such conduct must be reported, solely for the purpose of getting help. If the student is under the care of a psychiatrist, say that you will let him or her share the incident with that doctor.

EYE PROBLEMS

SEE ALSO
Disabilities, Physical
Health Problems
Tics

CAPSULE: Surprisingly, six out of ten schoolchildren who need eye attention are not getting it, or they are getting it too late! The popular eye-screening tests used in school are designed to test only the keenness or sharpness of what children see; they do not tell how well the children use their eyes or how well they see material near at hand. If you have concerns about students' eye capacities, consult an ophthalmologist or local agencies and service clubs that make sight saving their special concern.

Today, contact lenses and stylish eyeglasses have eased the problems of students who habitually lose glasses or resist wearing them because of vanity or inconvenience. Small children, however, still wear framed glasses and still have the usual problems of breaking them, misplacing them, and flatly refusing to wear them. Parents have a responsibility to apprise the teacher of their child's particular problem. School nurses can be helpful when eye exercises are required of the child during the school day.

Some children will show symptoms of eye problems—squinting, frowning, inattentiveness, losing their place, holding reading material too close to their face, or complaining of headaches. The teacher is responsible for sharing observation of these symptoms with people who can help.

O P T I O N S

1 Allow the child to wear a status symbol (such as a pretty "pin" or a special badge) if he or she will keep the glasses on. (Usually the child feels so much better, and sees so much more with glasses on that he or she is happy to wear them. The child who rebels may have glasses that are ill-fitted or frames that are too heavy, or may be using rebellion as a means of getting your attention.)

2 Check the print size of the child's study materials. Print that is too fine can put an undue burden on the child's eyes.

3 Comment on how nice the child looks in glasses.

4 Expect the child to wear the glasses. Delay beginning an activity until the child is ready, with glasses on.

5 Place the child with eye problems in a strategic place in the classroom so that he or she will not suffer eye strain.

6 Refer the child to the school nurse or a physician.

7 Reward the child when he or she wears the glasses. ("Maria has worn her glasses all day. Let's give her a hand!")

FEARFULNESS

SEE ALSO
Anxiety
School Phobia
Stress
Test Anxiety

CAPSULE: Some experienced and knowledgeable observers state that most student behavior in the classroom is based on fear, rather than on a desire to learn. Risk taking is dangerous in most classrooms. The "right/wrong" atmosphere that permeates some schools, and the consequences of either position, put stress on children—and an excessive amount on some. Many students spend their minutes in classrooms fearful of being called upon to recite or answer a question, of being wrong in reply, of what the teacher will do, of the other students making fun of them, of their parents hearing about their errors (or seeing their grades), of the punishment they may receive (or the privileges they may be denied), of actually being dumb, and so on. Some students are fearful both in and out of the classroom about whether others like them and about whether they will be included in activities, groups, or cliques.

Fears produce stress, and excessive stress immobilizes. However, immobilization is not always traumatic; it may be only fleeting. In fact, some stress is necessary for purposeful living, so our concern is the amount of fear and stress any one student is subjected to and how to deal with it. Our major effort must be to maximize the successful experiences for each child. Even then, there will be occasional wrongs, errors, or defeats. Negative teacher reactions, in the form of sarcasm, tirades, anger, and punishment, increase the stress and the resultant immobility; positive reactions, such as encouragement and assistance to the student, turn the failure into a learning experience.

OPTIONS

1 Be supportive when failures come. ("You're right in there, Seth, but we need to restudy the unit on fish. Try checking your answer against what you see in the aquarium.")

2 Commend consistently, but not effusively, any success of a fearful child.

3 Display appreciation of the capabilities of a fearful child. ("I couldn't help admiring the way you helped Laura during _____ when I knew you were just a little less scared yourself.") The student will learn, then, that you know he or she is struggling with fear.

4 Emphasize that "risk taking is free." Explain that every-

one fears failure (even the teacher) and that students must take risks in order to learn and grow.

5 Establish, if you can, the origin of the fear. Share your information discreetly so that the child may receive help.

6 Help the student develop friendships. Friends ameliorate the trauma of failure.

7 Match the difficulty and relevancy of subject matters and your requirements to the capabilities and interests of the student. (See Flight Plan, Appendix.)

8 Refer the student to the proper counseling service.

FIGHTING

SEE ALSO
Bullying

CAPSULE: When students cannot or choose not to resolve conflict by using words, they will often resort to physical fighting. Because teachers are responsible for the physical safety of their students (*in loco parentis*) as well as their academic development, fighting should be stopped quickly, or better, prevented. Prevent fights by establishing and repeating clearly articulated ground rules for behavior. Concentrate on setting a class climate in which kindness and mutual respect are the rule.

OPTIONS

1 Consider each student's involvement in a fight on an individual basis. Avoid treating the matter with anger and try to assign a consequence that fits the situation.

2 Have each fighter write his or her side of the story. If the student can't write, have that child draw a picture, dictate, or tape his or her side for you. Upon reading or listening to his or her own words, the student may reevaluate the situation.

3 Involve parents in discussing strategies to help students deal with anger and conflict constructively.

4 Isolate the fighters in a private room and hope for a joint, private resolution of their differences. Provide them with a tape recorder and an acceptable noise-maker, such as a drum, for dramatic sound effects. Don't insist upon a report unless they want to share the experience with you.

5 Refer students to the school disciplinarian, counselor, or principal (especially for more than a brief scuffle).

6 Use brainstorming to elicit creative ways to handle the urge to fight. ("In the next ten minutes let's share all the ways of resolving arguments or conflict without fighting.") (See Brainstorming, Appendix.)

7 Use the incident as a spring-board for discussion in a class meeting at a future time, when the incident has cooled and the fighters are more objective. (See Class Meeting, Appendix.)

8 Use the listing technique to help the student identify his or her feelings. ("List ten things that make you lose your temper," or "List ten things that used to make you angry.")

FORGETFULNESS

SEE ALSO
Truancy

CAPSULE: One who forgets habitually may be communicating: "I get attention by asking to borrow," "I'm stingy so I'll use others' materials," "I'm irresponsible." It's amazing how well people can remember to forget, especially if the consequences are gratifying. Establish in your classes sound habits of preparedness and reinforce the behavior of those who are trying to remember.

OPTIONS

1 Demonstrate that we must suffer the consequence of our own behavior. ("I'm sorry you forgot your gym shoes, but that means no basketball today.") *Caution:* Be aware that there are those who purposely forget so that they won't have to do a chore they fear or dislike. This calls for individual counseling and eventual facing up to such strategies.

2 Have a supply of stubby, eraserless pencils for the one who is always forgetting a pencil, and collect them at the end of the class.

3 Have the student maintain an assignment book. Initial the student's correct recording of the assignment. Ask the parent to initial the completed work.

4 Identify (via observation and repetition) the student who forgets because he or she fears or dislikes an assignment. ("Scott, I've noticed that you've forgotten your swim trunks three days in a row now. Something tells me you either don't like the water or don't like some people connected with swimming.")

5 Thank and reward the class for remembering. ("Thank you for remembering your donations to the Heart Fund. Since everyone remembered, let's treat ourselves to ten extra minutes on the volleyball court today!")

6 Use tangible reminders: a string around the wrist, a pinned-on note, polish on a fingernail, a note on a telegram blank, or a marble (which the student may keep) in a lunch pail to remind the child (and the mother). Why not give that child a second marble if he or she remembers? Or why not take something that belongs to the child and hold it in your "hockshop" until he or she remembers whatever was forgotten?

GAMBLING

SEE ALSO
Card Playing

CAPSULE: Although not a major activity in many schools, gambling is a problem in some schools. When students bet large sums of money on games of chance and run themselves into debt, they have a problem. Some educators think of compulsive gambling as an addiction similar to alcoholism. Especially if gambling becomes a habitual practice among some students in school, you might want to help them understand the scope of the problem and some control mechanisms.

OPTIONS

1 Assign a research project through which students learn some of the causes and effects of compulsive gambling.

2 Hold class discussions about gambling covering the legal ramifications, school rules, and consequences. (See Class Discussions, Appendix.)

3 Investigate self-help groups, such as Gamblers Anonymous.

4 Involve students thoroughly in academics and extracurricular activities so that a void does not exist which could be filled by gambling.

SEE ALSO
Drinking
Dropouts
Drug Use
Name Slurring
Vandalism

GANGS

CAPSULE: Although youth gangs are not a new phenomenon, during recent years they have expanded nationwide and have taken on alarming new behaviors. Gangs have extended past large city boundaries and have infiltrated suburban and even rural communities. Legally, a youth gang is defined as an organized group involved in criminal activity. In practice, group members often display disrespect for established authority and conventional morality. School-related gang activity may include drug abuse, intimidation, harassment, graffiti, vandalism, and theft.

Young people often join gangs because they feel as if they do not belong anywhere else. A gang can offer students status, protection, and an immediate peer group. The breakdown of the nuclear family, low self-esteem, peer pressure, and lack of success in school are some of the reasons students join gangs.

Because gangs are easier to prevent than to eliminate, school personnel must be alert to the beginning signs of gang activity. A policy for dealing with gang activity needs to be in place before gangs become prevalent in the school. Administrators, teachers, and parents must work together to diminish gang activity in order to provide a safe learning environment for children.

OPTIONS

1 Check for gang symbols, such as graffiti, earrings, hats, or ornaments. Look for symbols within students' names. For example, a pitchfork is a common symbol; the spelling of a name such as "LUIS" as "LUIS" should be viewed as possibly symptomatic.

2 Communicate openly with parents. Educate them about gang activity and prevention, in general, and about any suspicious activity involving their own children.

3 Develop a drug and gang prevention program in which students learn decision-making, self-expression and coping skills. Strengthen students' sense of self and belonging so that they will not be vulnerable to gang pressure.

4 Establish the school and the classroom as a "neutral turf," a protected area where no threats, intimidation, or buying and selling can take place.

5 Look for strange vehicles on the school campus and for nonstudent young people in school. Permit only authorized visitors in school.

6 Provide a strong extracurricular program. Encourage each student to become involved in at least one activity. Students' involvement in extracurricular activities provides a sense of belonging and allows less time for "hanging around," when students can be approached by gang members.

7 Sensitize all members of the school community to multicultural issues. Encourage ethnic pride through classroom activities and the arts. Help students achieve success through school so that they do not establish identity through gang affiliation.

8 Work constructively with local law enforcement agencies. Maintain contact with the police regarding gang activity and cooperate with the prosecution of destructive youth.

GIFTED CHILDREN

SEE ALSO
Culturally Diverse

CAPSULE: All children are "gifted." If any doubt or uncertainty exists about this indisputable "fact," just ask their parents. In recent years a multitude of definitions of gifted behavior has emerged, ranging from "multiple talents" to "overexcitabilities." Common sense and experience reveal that in any classroom, whether students are grouped heterogeneously or homogeneously, a variety of aptitudes will emerge. Teachers and parents should capitalize on those aptitudes by providing challenging, enriching educational opportunities.

OPTIONS

1 Avoid labeling. Definitions and guidelines for gifted behavior are elusive. Attempting to classify one group (or even an individual) as "gifted" may be a foolish endeavor. Treat students as individuals and appeal to their strengths, whatever they may be.

2 Construct assignments and activities on varied levels of complexity. Recognize diversity within the classroom and provide appropriately challenging work for all students. (See Flight Plan, Appendix.)

3 Create an open-ended program if the state or school mandates a special program for gifted students. Use at least three criteria (different kinds of assessments) to identify gifted behaviors. Allow students (whether or not they qualify officially) to participate in special programs on the basis of interest and desire.

4 Encourage creativity through assignments that allow students to compose and invent works of art and products. Help students to submit their work to publishers and contests for recognition.

5 Nurture students' tendencies to question, doubt, and challenge others' thinking.

GOSSIP

SEE ALSO
Tattling

CAPSULE: Gossip is usually a report of an intimate nature that includes some sensational facts. While tattling, so common among younger children, usually deals with trivialities like "Somebody took my chair," or "He pushed me," gossip flourishes among older students and is frequently related to sex, drugs, pregnancies, sexually transmitted diseases, wild parties, gambling, theft, abortions, incest, and gangs. The effects of malicious gossip can be devastating.

The most effective gossip deterrent is unwillingness to listen to or to repeat malicious comments about another. Teachers, exposed to the stormy overtones of gossip problems in school, walk a fine line that separates the *indifferent,* who just "don't want to become involved" at any price, and the *different,* who temper information thrust their way with common sense and care enough to become involved if the situation demands or warrants it.

O P T I O N S

1 Ask the gossip if he or she is willing to put into writing the juicy morsel just peddled to you.

2 Expect students to be positive, instead of negative, in their comments about others. Hopefully, the attitude generated in class will spill over into the students' purely social contacts.

3 Help students, through class discussions (see Appendix), learn how to cope with gossip when they are the ones gossiped about. They will be able to add to these suggestions: Ignore the gossip, refrain from countercharging, talk to someone you can trust, and don't talk to everyone.

4 Play the old gossip game, with students whispering to their neighbors what they think they heard from the ones next to them. The end product carries its own message.

5 Resist the temptation to get "in on" the gossip that you sense is going around. Promptly discount 90 percent of what you overhear and put the other 10 percent into mental cold storage, just in case it proves significant later on.

6 Role play situations that involve gossip. Through skits identify problems caused by gossip. Discuss the consequences of gossip. (See Role Playing, Appendix.)

GRADES

CAPSULE: Few would argue that assessment and evaluation are a necessary part of education. However, when an evaluation system creates a great deal of stress and de-emphasizes the learning process, teachers and parents must question its validity. A rigid grading system may cause psychological burdens and may not motivate true academic achievement.

Some elementary schools have moved away from letter and number marking systems to narrative reports, sometimes accompanied by parent conferences. Using individualized written and oral assessments as a framework, parents, teachers, and students can discuss academic progress in concrete and meaningful ways. In secondary schools, grades and class rank are used to help determine students' post-high-school options. Grades help colleges compare students, one to another, in a highly competitive selection process. The pressure caused by the grading system is inevitable; however, teachers and parents can work together to alleviate some of the stress.

O P T I O N S

1 Create "alternative" assessment opportunities, such as
portfolios of students' best
work. In this authentic
assessment model (see
Appendix), students evaluate their own work using
developed criteria. A teacher
assessment follows student
evaluation, making assessment a joint process.

2 De-emphasize the notion of
the "bell-shaped curve." In
presenting an evaluation
system, tell students that
everyone *can* earn an "A."
Do not limit high grades to a
certain number of students
or insist that a certain per-
centage of students must
fail. Set high academic standards and state explicitly
that all students are capable
of receiving good grades.

3 Encourage parents of a
grade-obsessed child to seek
family counseling. The child
who frequently breaks down
over the difference between
a "B+" and an "A-" may be
receiving unduly stressful
messages from home.
Sometimes parents are
unaware of the effects of
their messages and expectations.

4 Individualize the lessons
using the Flight Plan (see
Appendix). The fact that the
student begins with a unit
that eliminates failure by
immediately guaranteeing at
least a "D" is an incentive to
the chronic failer.

5 Reward effort as well as
achievement. Reduce the
fear of failure by reassuring
students that everyone who
works and completes all
assignments will attain some
success.

GUM CHEWING

CAPSULE: Teacher acceptance of gum chewing varies considerably. Gum can be a distinct menace, a minor annoyance, or no trouble at all in the classroom. If you are employed in a school where rules flatly state the expectations regarding gum, you must simply enforce the rules. If you are operating in a more relaxed setting, perhaps some of the following ideas will be helpful.

O P T I O N S

1 Consider gum chewing as one way of coping with stress and permit it during exams, with the provision that the student does not crack gum and/or chomp to the annoyance of others.

2 Inform the students that among your peculiarities is an abhorrence of gum chewing. Solicit their abstinence from this distracting behavior.

3 Inform the students that your main concern is that learning take place in a conducive environment. Unless they pose obstructions to that ideal, nothing need be said about gum chewing or any other disturbance.

4 Take a common-sense approach. Inform students that they may chew gum as long as you neither see nor hear it. The moment chewing is visible or audible, students must spit out the gum. If a repeated pattern occurs, deny the student(s) gum-chewing privileges on a permanent basis.

HALITOSIS

SEE ALSO
Body Odors

CAPSULE: Halitosis is the scientific name for bad breath. Normal exhaled air has a faint smell that is not offensive. Halitosis, on the other hand, is of great social significance, as borne out by the money spent on gargles and breath mints. People everywhere shy away from the person with halitosis, especially in crowded places, such as the classroom where close contact is unavoidable.

The causes of halitosis are twofold: those of intra-oral origin, that is from the mouth itself, and those from areas other than the mouth. The most significant causes of halitosis are those that occur in the mouth. Poor oral hygiene allows food debris to collect and stagnate and contributes greatly to bad odors, as do dental decay, oral infection, and smoking. Certain foods with high garlic or onion content are soon detected on the breath. Regular visits to the dentist are recommended for the removal of plaque, a chief culprit in causing halitosis. Extra-oral causes of bad breath include tonsillitis, lung infections, and malignant tumors.

O P T I O N S

1 Be mindful of your own breath, for you work closely with the students. "Smoker's breath" can adversely affect anyone, child or adult, who must come in close contact with a smoker. Discuss with colleagues the inadvisability of smoking before school or during breaks.

2 Deal with problems involving bad breath with extreme tact. A child who is once

labeled as "a stink mouth" doesn't soon forget it.

3 Promote and discuss general cleanliness directly and indirectly in your work area.

4 Refer a student with halitosis to a member of your counseling staff who will know about the agencies in your community that volunteer dental work for low-income families.

HANDEDNESS

CAPSULE: The matter of handedness is less a concern these days than it was during the period of the widely touted cerebral-dominance theory, which seems to be receding into obscurity. By the time a child enters school, he or she will have a well-developed preference for one hand or the other. You will occasionally encounter an ambidextrous student.

OPTIONS

1 Accord left-handed students a few common courtesies, including: (1) seating them so that their left hands don't bump their neighbors' right hands during writing lessons or examinations, (2) seating them judiciously at the lunch table for the same reason, (3) showing them how to place their papers in the correct position so that they won't be forced to develop a crabbed way of writing, and (4) having left-handed scissors for their use.

2 Permit left-handed children to follow their natural inclinations.

HEALTH PROBLEMS

SEE ALSO
AIDS
Allergies

CAPSULE: When confronted with health problems, resist the temptation to diagnose ills and prescribe remedies. Parents, school medical staff, and the student's family physician will value your keen observations and accurate reports of the child's symptoms. You will be among the first to note signs of epidemic illnesses such as measles, mumps, chicken pox, conjunctivitis and impetigo. You will be in a prime position to note significant clues to previously undetected or unidentified ills, the signs of which might be extreme drowsiness, fatigue, coughing, dizziness, pallor, stumbling and falling, or hyperactivity. Furthermore, you will be in a position to identify the kinds of activities that create anxiety or that provoke allergy or asthma attacks.

For your own benefit, review carefully the health records of each of your students. In addition to physical ills, you may become aware of certain psychological ills.

Masochism and sadism are sometimes evidenced in children's behaviors. Signs of the former include pain-inspired anxiety that becomes pleasurable and is directed toward the self. Signs of the latter include the anxiety-pleasurable sequence, directed toward others. Both behavior types have perverse and desexualized forms and contain three major elements: fantasy, suspense, and demonstrativeness. The teacher often finds the idea that a child could strive for physical or psychic pain difficult to accept. Behavior of this quality is aberrational and, like all extreme, deviant, or bizarre behaviors that are persistent, should be referred to psychological and/or psychiatric personnel.

Beyond recognizing significant signs and alerting the family, as well as alerting professionals who can diagnose and treat, you sometimes have the added responsibility of "standing in" until medical help arrives. Your school administrator will apprise you of prevailing schoolwide health and accident procedures. Ask the school nurse to review safety measures and health rules with your students. Here are some security measures you may take in your own classroom.

O P T I O N S

1 Arrange the seating for the maximum comfort and convenience of all. For instance, seat the child with a brace or a crutch in an uncluttered area; the chronic hiccupper near the door for ready access to the drinking fountain; the farsighted, nearsighted, and hearing impaired in advantageous spots; and the student with a kidney problem close to the door.

2 Consider children with health problems when planning large-group testing, field trips, and excursions. Don't always think first of "sending them to the library." Be more creative than that! School specialists can be of enormous help in this regard.

3 Make a "backstop" arrangement with another teacher or a student whereby emergencies can be met if you are away from the scene. ("If Brian has a seizure, you should . . . .") Caution: Sometimes parents of the helping child resent your placing that much responsibility on him or her, so obtain clearance from both students' families. Instill in all the students an attitude of caring, without chaos.

4 Refer sick students to school medical personnel.

5 Use the school nurse or physician as a resource person. Remember, they are educators, too! Learning to take proper care of one's body is basic to other kinds of learning.

HEARING PROBLEMS

SEE ALSO
Acting Out
Health Problems

CAPSULE: School health programs provide some services for screening students for hearing problems. However, due to circumstances not always under the control of the system, many weeks may pass before students are tested. Each teacher must learn early in the semester which students may have hearing problems. Some students act out because they can't hear what others are saying. Others withdraw because they don't want to call attention to their condition. The observant teacher will notice the child who tilts his or her head to favor a certain ear, or the one who talks to fill the void. The teacher can use simple tests to identify those who may have difficulty hearing (see Option 3).

OPTIONS

1 Consult the parents or guardian regarding a child's health history if you suspect a hearing impairment.

2 Face the child when speaking to him or her.

3 Give a sample hearing test yourself, if no medical staff is available. Place the student twenty feet from you, with one ear toward you. Ask the student to cover the other ear with one hand. Pronounce words, phrases, numbers, and letters in a wide range of intensity. Ask the student to raise the free hand when he or she hears your voice. Repeat the procedure for the other ear, then for both ears.

4 Place the student close to the front of the room so that he or she can see the face of the teacher and can lipread.

5 Refer the student to the school medical staff or outside services for screening.

HOMESICKNESS

CAPSULE: Homesickness is the natural longing for family, friends, and familiar routines that people experience when they are away from home for extended periods of time. For younger children, homesickness can occur at boarding schools or overnight camps. For older students, the first major case of homesickness may take place when they leave home to attend college or to pursue other post-secondary options.

Astute camp and boarding school directors are aware of the symptoms (moroseness, loss of appetite, general malaise) and take a proactive approach to minimize homesickness. They make special plans for times of the day or week when children might feel most vulnerable: bedtime, Sundays, stormy days or nights, or visiting days when some children receive no visitors.

Parents can also help minimize homesickness by holding a discussion on the topic before children leave home. Children must know that their lonely feelings are natural and, with good luck, sporadic. They should also know that involvement in activities with peers may be the best cure for the homesick "blues."

O P T I O N S

1 Allow students to make a designated number of phone calls during a certain period. Permit exceptions only in the case of an emergency.

2 Assign tasks that require attentiveness to the job and merit commendations by others if the job is well done. ("Jason, would you and Gina prepare wood for the bonfire?")

3 Encourage parents to write cheerful, positive, matter-of-fact letters. Letters that stress how much the child is missed or how much the child is missing by not being

home may cause or aggravate homesickness.

4 Keep students busy with group activities that nurture friendships and help them discover unexpected facets of their personalities. Good humor and the unexpected can help dispel tears.

5 Provide time for one-to-one chats between camp or school personnel and young people. Sometimes the best treatment for homesickness is the knowledge that someone cares enough to talk and to listen.

HOMEWORK

SEE ALSO
Procrastination

C A P S U L E : "Not until you've done your homework!" is a conditional pronouncement that has a familiar ring to many students. "I have to finish my homework!" is a familiar response to a parental request.

What is homework and how can it be dealt with satisfactorily? We believe homework should be purposeful activity, not busywork, and that it has two functions: It should provide needed practice in a skill well taught by the teacher and it should reinforce concepts learned.

While it is sometimes difficult to remain detached, parents are wise to allow children to be responsible to the teacher for their homework. Too much parental assistance can be disastrous to both students and parents. Teachers should communicate their homework expectations to the parents. "Lost" or "forgotten" papers often create classroom and home conflicts. The following ideas for parents and teachers may be helpful.

O P T I O N S

1 Ask each student to keep a well-identified folder or a notebook with pockets to hold loose papers.

2 Begin the homework assignment, occasionally, during the end of the regular class period to allow for clarification or questions before students are dismissed.

3 Create a homework haven in the home, with good lighting, comfortable seating, and few distractions. Give the student a choice regarding when to do homework: before or after dinner. Help set up and maintain a regular schedule and place for homework.

4 Have each student maintain an assignment book that parents may also refer to, if necessary.

5 Make sure that students understand the importance of homework by checking and/or evaluating their work.

HOMOSEXUALITY

CAPSULE: Homosexuality is an orientation that has been regarded throughout history by different cultures in different ways. Today in the United States, sexual orientation is a subject that makes many people uneasy. This sensitive topic has an impact particularly on teenagers, who may be confused about their personal orientation.

Experts espouse theories regarding the causes of homosexuality ranging from physical to cultural. Although no one theory has been accepted as "gospel," the current AIDS epidemic (which knows no sexual boundaries) has led to misinformation and the resulting "homophobia." School is an ideal place for students to receive factual, objective information so that fear and prejudice do not exacerbate an already potentially volatile situation. Teachers can emphasize and model respect for all people. Students should learn that persecuting others, for any reason, is neither right nor just.

OPTIONS

1 Be mindful that confused youth who are trying to sort out their sexual orientation may be at risk for other problems such as drug and alcohol abuse, suicide, or mental illness.

2 Consult the school counselor as a source for positive intervention with adolescents who question their sexual feelings.

3 Keep abreast of the subject through professional journals so that you are well informed when dealing with students. Combat prejudice and misinformation with straight talk and facts.

4 Request, if a program is not already available, the education of teachers and parents on ways to address the subject of homosexuality.

HYPERACTIVITY *HYPERKINESIS*

SEE ALSO
Acting Out
Attention Deficit Disorder
Attention Span

CAPSULE: Hyperactivity is characterized by the inability to focus in different environments. The hyperactive child often displays excessive movement, such as foot or hand tapping. Hyperactive children also exhibit a general appearance of anxiety. Sleep disturbances, causing tiredness, and inattentiveness due to the inability to focus often result in learning gaps. Additionally, a hyperactive child's excessive motor activity may create distractions for other students.

O P T I O N S :

1 Break tasks down into small, manageable components. Give the child a rest coupled with positive reinforcement after each component is completed.

2 Conduct an evaluation through the special services of the school or an outside agency. Individual or family counseling may be recommended.

3 Create the most structured environment possible at home and at school. Try to limit the amount of stimulation the child receives (auditory, visual, kinesthetic, etc.). Set up a routine for the child's activities at home, such as a certain time and place for homework and a meal schedule.

4 Encourage the family to take the student to a doctor who can test for hyperactivity. A blood chemistry test can determine whether medication might be helpful.

5 Give hyperactive students specific classroom responsibilities, such as taking attendance. Classroom tasks make students feel important and allow them legitimate opportunities to move out of their seats.

6 Share concerns with others in the school community. Teachers can share diagnostic information and strategies with each other. Parents can join a support group where they can express feelings without embarrassment.

HYPOCHONDRIA

SEE ALSO
Health Problems

CAPSULE: The hypochondriac persistently worries about illness, even though no physical symptoms may be present. The anxiety level may become so great that the student becomes dysfunctional in school. Hypochondriacs may use imagined physical distress to draw attention to themselves or to remove themselves from unpleasant or stressful situations (such as tests). Hypochondria may signal an underlying problem that requires medical or psychological diagnosis.

OPTIONS:

1 Alert the school medical staff. Leave the physical diagnosis and treatment recommendations to them, unless they enlist your aid.

2 Consult with other teachers and parents to determine the nature of the "illness" pattern. A need for attention or inappropriate responses to stress may be a cause.

3 Create an action plan with other professionals and parents. Once "real" physical symptoms have been discounted by professionals, gently insist that the student participate and follow through in school activities.

4 Meet with the student and practice active listening. Repeat some of the student's concerns back to the source, and try to hear what the student is not saying—the real cause of the imagined physical distress.

IMMORAL BEHAVIOR

SEE ALSO
Cheating
Lying
Stealing

CAPSULE: The notion of an "innate conscience" is often called into question. With changes in the family structure, the effectiveness of moral training in the home is also called into question. Some people feel that because of a general lack of moral training, sociopathic behavior is on the rise and many young people simply do not know the difference between right and wrong. While moral education is not the exclusive province of the classroom teacher, ethical standards and behaviors can be taught and modeled within the context of an academic environment.

OPTIONS

1 Emphasize consequences for unethical behavior through the study of current events. Discuss news events in which high-profile people who act in unethical ways (cheating on taxes, etc.) lose assets and often end up in prison. (See Class Discussions, Appendix.)

2 Model fair and ethical behavior in front of students. Be kind and just with students so that they have an example to follow.

3 Provide group decision-making opportunities in which students need to choose a course of action. Furnish situations in which students must ask themselves, "What is the right way?"

4 Select literature and other text material that include examples of moral dilemmas. Relate issues in textual material to issues in students' own lives.

INSUBORDINATION

SEE ALSO
Acting Out
Baiting the Teacher

CAPSULE: Students who are insubordinate are unwilling to submit to authority. They fight against those whom they perceive wield power. Often the struggle takes place in disruptive, attention-getting ways.

Teachers and parents should avoid power struggles with these children by establishing atmospheres of consistency. Adults should attempt to find out causes of the behavior. Does the insurbordinate child merely seek attention? Does the student seek revenge for a perceived injustice? Has the teacher been overly informal or authoritarian? Teachers and parents may refer the child for counseling, formal or informal.

OPTIONS:

1 Have the insurbordinate student report to someone (teacher, counselor, social worker, etc.) on a regular basis. The student should report any behavioral change from one visit to the next. The student should serve as an introspective reporter; the adult should serve as an active listener.

2 Help the student to interpret his or her goals. Use win/win communication techniques. "Let's brainstorm about ways in which we can work together."

3 Isolate the student until you have time to talk on a one-to-one basis. Deal with the student individually, in a friendly, nonconfrontational manner.

4 Perform a surprise act of kindness. Praising the student for a minor achievement may be disarming.

5 Use a face-saver for a first offense. "What you did just came across as disrespectful, but I'm sure you didn't mean it that way."

6 Use a three-step procedure for treating insubordinate behavior: First offense: a conference; second offense: a privilege revoked; third offence: notification of parents through administrative channels.

IRRESPONSIBILITY

SEE ALSO
Carelessness
Forgetfulness
Self-Concept

CAPSULE: Working with responsible individuals helps life go smoothly. Responsible people bring to tasks an interest, a willingness to tackle the job, and a sense of caring, as well as an understanding of what assignments entail and a realistic concept (self-concept) of their ability to meet the demands of the job. Commitment and maturity are characteristics of a responsible person.

Irresponsible people are more than careless. They often come on strong at first, giving an air of confidence, even sincerity, but do not seem to know how to follow through. Retraining by establishing realistic consequences can be accomplished but is difficult once behavior patterns are set.

OPTIONS

1 Allow students to experience the natural consequences of irresponsible behavior. Students who forget to bring their musical instruments to school cannot play in the orchestra; students who repeatedly forget to do or bring homework to school receive low grades. Avoid enabling behaviors—taking on the responsibility of another person.

2 Confront the irresponsible student directly, without rancor, explaining that word is getting around about the behavior. ("Bill, on three occasions within the past two months you have volunteered to lead important committees, and in each case you fell short of the mark. Your credibility is being questioned. I think I know some ways that you can regain the confidence of your classmates. Drop by my office this week, and we'll talk about it.")

3 Convey to the student the message that a responsible person is independent and that an irresponsible one remains dependent, a sign of immaturity. Being immature is the last thing a student wants to be!

4 Give bite-sized lessons or tasks and expect acceptable completion of them before allowing the student to progress to the next phase. (See Flight Plan, Appendix.)

5 Reward with honest, verbal praise the student who demonstrates responsibility. Emphasize some specific competence, not just competence in general. ("Rusty, your committee's plan for the prom is so clear that it is easy to visualize the event," rather than, "You've got a great committee there; I'm sure you'll do a great job!") Clinch the feeling of success by having students tell you why they think they succeeded.

6 Use an extrinsic reward to motivate the student. Try the self-management record (see Appendix), noting that the items listed relate to responsibility. In using this approach students readily learn that they reap the consequences of their behavior and that any group of people can be sorted into two subgroups, the responsible and the irresponsible.

ISOLATED CHILDREN

SEE **ALSO**
Anxiety
Rejected Children

CAPSULE: Isolated children live on the fringes of their social environment. Hungry to be accepted and part of the mainstream, they try to become part of the group. Often their attempts are met with painful rejection. Isolated students find peer interaction difficult; they are frequently misunderstood and sometimes never given a chance by other students. Middle school/junior high can be exceptionally difficult years for students who find themselves apart from others.

OPTIONS

1 Connect the isolated student with a better accepted child through the "buddy" system. Pair students to share homework information and absence make-up responsibilities.

2 Create group projects so that isolated children have the opportunity to interact with others during class. Assign group homework so that the interaction extends beyond school hours.

3 Discuss the problem and potential solutions with parents.

4 Examine the child's file. Is being socially isolated a longstanding pattern? Is it related to appearance, odor, or behavior? What strategies have been attempted to alleviate the problem? Consider referring the student to another professional staff member for counseling.

5 Try bibliotherapy (see Appendix).

JEALOUSY

SEE ALSO
Sibling Rivalry

CAPSULE: Jealousy is generally the product of feelings of inferiority or a sense that others are being favored. Feelings of inferiority come from constant reminders (real or implied) that others are better, more competent, or superior. Feelings of favoritism come when one must share time and attention or give them up to another. A new student in the class, a new teacher on the faculty, or a new baby in the home can stir emotions students didn't realize they had. The overly jealous student eyes any newcomer as a threat and expresses jealousy in hostile ways, often against the very person whose affection is in question.

Forever placating the jealous one can be a strain as well as an exercise in futility. The focus should be on promoting healthy attitudes which will diminish the emotion until the child has a better understanding. Active listening and wise redirection of actions are implicit in the following suggestions.

OPTIONS

1 Allow the child to express jealousy in a noninjurious manner. For example, ask the student to show you feelings about the rival through handling an inanimate object, such as a piece of play dough or clay, or a stuffed toy.

2 Elicit from the child concrete examples of favoritism using "what" and "how" as keys. ("Let's talk about what Mrs. S. does that makes you think she favors Jan over you," or "Let's see if you can show me how Mrs. S. favors Jan.") Note: Refrain from asking "why" because the typical answer will be "I don't know." However, with the very young a "why" question can provide an opportunity for you to ask, "Will you let me tell you what I think about it?"

3 Empathize with the child. ("I know how you feel. I used to feel that my mother preferred to have my sister serve the cookies when guests came. However, I remember now that she preferred to have me entertain the visitors' children because she said I was so responsible.")

4 Talk about emotions in class: "Jealousy is sometimes called the green-eyed monster. I wonder why," or "What do you think of this statement: There are two kinds of people and they look at life in mathematical terms—either they think others are out to subtract from or divide up their lot, or they are multiplying and adding to it."

KICKING AND HITTING

SEE ALSO
Acting Out
Anger
Fighting

CAPSULE: Kicking and hitting are convenient, natural responses to something in a person's way—our arms and legs are always ready on a moment's notice. The child who resorts to kicking and hitting will eventually be forced by society to wield more subtle weapons, but between the ages of three and nine these behaviors may satisfy the need to get attention, to seek revenge, or to show who is tough and powerful. Persistent aggressiveness reflects feelings of worthlessness. Teachers and parents must guide such students toward more acceptable behavior.

OPTIONS

1 Encourage students to use words to express feelings. Insist that in the safe environment of the classroom, any physical violence is unacceptable.

2 Give students opportunities for productive physical activity. These may serve as a release for physical tension.

3 Isolate the physically aggressive student until you can have a one-on-one talk. Try to elicit the underlying reasons for kicking and hitting. Pay attention to whether the student is seeking revenge, feeling threatened and scared, or wants attention. Your approach will depend upon the student's motivations.

4 Remove the student from the group for a "time out." Provide an opportunity for the student to recover composure and to reflect on the notion that causing others physical pain cannot be tolerated.

LATCHKEY CHILDREN

SEE ALSO
Loneliness

CAPSULE: Latchkey children are left on their own or in the care of a brother or sister under fourteen years of age for long periods of time. Some experts estimate that 25 percent of school-age children of working parents care for themselves regularly.

These children have a common set of concerns and experiences. Their fears range from assault to fear of storms, fire, and noises. Many parents are comfortable trusting their young children to fend for themselves and establish strict rules (no friends in the house, no telephoning) until an adult gets home. The school and the home can work together to assist these children.

OPTIONS

1 Discuss, in small groups, fears and coping strategies children have when left alone.

2 Inform parents of any existing after-school care programs and call-in lines that provide help in emergencies or just listen to a worried or lonely child.

3 Investigate starting before- and after-school care programs through the school or through another agency, such as the park district.

LICE

CAPSULE: These flat, sluggish, wingless arthropods select the fanciest of homes for themselves—the heads of humans. Children sometimes come to school with lice; sometimes they pick them up from their playmates, especially if they are in the habit of sharing their combs, brushes, barrettes, or hair ribbons.

One of the first signs of lice is itchiness and excessive head scratching. Another is the sight of tiny grayish-white clusters—the eggs of lice.

Many school health programs are equipped to eradicate lice with proper delousing applications. The problem of getting at the source, which may be among family members not in school, is a constant one. If possible, treat the entire family household. To accomplish this may require the finesse of a top-level public relations officer.

OPTIONS

1 Discuss parasites as part of a regular class lesson. Mention lice. Encourage students who suspect they may have lice to have the nurse check their heads. Open discussion and matter-of-fact handling of the problem may discourage rejection of the child with lice by classmates.

2 Encourage the children to refrain from sharing their combs and other personal items. Have a supply of clean combs to sell or give the children with the understanding that they will not share. Provide special "lice combs" and shampoos.

3 Send the student to the school health department as soon as you see evidence of lice. (If your school has inadequate health facilities,

see your administrator about establishing a better procedure for dealing with health and hygiene matters.)

4 Use filmstrips or slides to teach students about contagion and parasites.

LISTENING PROBLEMS

SEE ALSO
Attention Span
Hearing Problems

CAPSULE: Listening is an art that requires thought and attentiveness; it is not to be confused with hearing, the power of perceiving sound. Many feel that listening is fast becoming one of the "lost arts" and that hearing among youth is suffering the ill effects of amplified electronic sounds. In addition to suffering from overly amplified music, young people are also affected by the "sound-byte syndrome," in which information is presented in mini-segments for short attention spans.

Students learn to be good or poor listeners from their adult models. Teachers need to model active listening and to give ample opportunity for students to initiate communication. Each student's contribution needs to be protected. The old model of the teacher as the "sage on the stage" and of students as passive sponges soaking up knowledge is defunct.

Most of us can afford to hone listening skills a bit. Ideally, from observing the teacher as a good listener, students will learn to empathize with others, to catch significant overtones expressed by the speaker, and to be less self-centered. In a good listening environment, information can be shared in a productive, meaningful way.

OPTIONS

1 Establish a class routine that involves beginning a period of the day with a listening-skill builder. For instance, you might select a brief article (not more than 200 words) to read to the class once. Follow the reading with five to ten comprehension questions. Correct the answers immediately and chart the results on individual graphs. A possible variation: ask students to select and administer the listening test.

2 Give directions a limited number of times. Much poor listening is perpetuated by teachers' willingness, despite annoyance, to repeat things innumerable times.

3 Play games that require careful listening. Several games require that each student recall, not only what the previous speaker said, but also what the one before that said, and the one before that. Listening and memory training, then, go hand in hand. Consult library books for appropriate games to encourage better listening.

4 Teach students listening skills and pitfalls. (See Appendix.)

5 Use riddles to capture the students' attention before moving into a problem that requires careful listening.

LITTERING

SEE ALSO
Carelessness
Irresponsibility
Messiness

CAPSULE: In a time when environmental awareness is stressed in schools everywhere, schools struggle daily with the problem of litter. Students who feel that a custodial staff is employed to pick up after them are just as misguided as the administrators who close their eyes to the care of the buildings and grounds. A first-time visitor can, by a casual stroll through the halls and a stop-off in a washroom, quickly discern the morale level of a school. Litter, graffiti, and filth proliferate in a climate where indifference (and perhaps incompetence) dwells. A schoolwide campaign to build pride in surroundings can be a first step in eliminating (or significantly lessening) litter.

OPTIONS

1 Conduct a no-litter campaign. Sell bumper stickers or notebook stickers. Offer prizes for the best slogan, poster, skit, or song on the subject of litter.

2 Encourage pride in the appearance of the school by recognizing individuals or classes for outstanding efforts to keep the school clean. This may be done through a morning bulletin, the intercom system, or at an assembly program.

3 Introduce the custom of having student guides take visitors around the school. This helps the students become aware of the appearance of the school and generates pride in it.

4 Schedule students, as a consequence of littering, for outdoor litter pickup.

5 Use environmental protection as a subject for discussion, writing, and speaking in the appropriate subject classes, such as social studies, English, or speech.

LONELINESS

SEE ALSO
Anxiety
Homesickness
Withdrawn Children

C A P S U L E : Loneliness has many causes, but at the heart of the problem is someone's inability to relate well to others. Because of low self-esteem and a lack of social skills, an individual fails to connect with others. That failure to connect and rejection by others worsens the self-esteem problem. The person becomes increasingly isolated; it's a vicious circle.

Children must have people to relate to in order to grow and develop properly. In schools today, students are sometimes not only lonely, but are lost and lonely. Teachers are in a position to reach out and provide caring and company for lonely children.

O P T I O N S

1 Arrange for the lonely student to tutor a student in a lower grade or to work with a student in the same grade on a project. Being assigned to work with another will provide the opportunity to relate in a nonthreatening way.

2 Create group assignments and projects in which students must relate to one another over a period of time, both in school and at home.

3 Encourage students to express themselves through creative activities, such as songs, poems or pictures, which correspond to their feelings. In keeping a daily journal, themes or recurring patterns of loneliness may become evident, providing fodder for discussion.

4 Generate communication among students who are not yet acquainted. Play "treasure hunt" games in which students must find each other through descriptors.

5 Send the lonely student on errands with one other child. Sometimes getting away from the group can help an individual make personal contact.

6 Show students appreciation through compliments and positive reinforcement. The more self-esteem is built, the easier making contact will be.

LYING

SEE ALSO
Anxiety
Stealing

CAPSULE: Lying is as old as Eden. Practiced enough, it becomes reflexive. Generally, lying springs from feelings of inadequacy and pressure.

Adults sometimes fail to recognize that there are gradations of truth and falsehoods and that age groups view them differently. The very young child often can't differentiate between fantasy and reality. Also, parents and teachers sometimes make truth-telling difficult, as in the case of the student who told his teacher he hated his grandmother, only to be scolded and called a "bad" boy. In the interest of expediency, he turned to saying things that pleased his teacher and made himself a "good" liar.

Threats are poor deterrents to lying. Calling the untruthful child a liar doesn't help either. Dealing with lying is usually an uphill undertaking that requires patience, consistency, and maybe some professional help.

OPTIONS

1 Appeal to the student's self-opinion. Use "I" messages. ("I feel unhappy when you don't tell the truth because I've always liked being able to count on what you say.")

2 Arrange for the student who lies to be paired with a more truthful child when working on class projects. A good model may be helpful in changing behavior.

3 Assure children that they can depend upon you to tell the truth. Provide a strong, personal role model.

4 Deal directly with students who lie instead of trying to trap them.

5 Evaluate your expectations of students and try to discern the areas in which they feel compelled to lie. Do they, for example, lie about schoolwork? Their parents' jobs? Their material possessions? Their physical prowess?

6 Present a hypothetical or real instance of lying for class reaction. For example: "A few years ago I had in my class three girls who were caught shoplifting in the dime store. Two people saw them taking lipstick and gum, and the store manager even presented a picture of one of the girls putting lipstick in her purse. Yet, each girl denied taking anything. How would you handle this?" Such a discussion often begins with retributive solutions and winds up looking at why the girls felt moved to steal and then lie about it. A simple, "Have you ever found yourself locked into a similar situation?" sometimes elicits some interesting exchanges.

7 Read or tell stories that illustrate the power of truthfulness over falsehoods. Resist the temptation to moralize; let the students discern the implications.

8 Recognize and reinforce positive truth-telling. ("I'm sure it was difficult for you to admit you forgot to tell your dad to call me last night, but I'm so proud of you for admitting it." The assumption here is that the teacher and the student recognize the problem and are both working on it.)

9 Use normal consequences to help the student learn the benefits of telling the truth. ("You said you had finished _____ and it's clear you didn't tell the truth, so you will be unable to attend _____ .")

MASTURBATION

CAPSULE: Masturbation is a normal phenomenon in the process of self-discovery. In Western culture, this practice in public generates considerable concern and embarrassment. A preschooler may masturbate, quite unaware that the act carries any social disapproval. Older children masturbating in school or public places could be showing signs of emotional problems. Do confront the problem because public masturbation causes discomfort in any social situation.

OPTIONS

1 Change the activity of the class. Play a record, for instance, and tell the children to march or dance.

2 Check the child's clothing. Is it too tight and perhaps irritating?

3 Check with the parents and recommend that they seek help from a physician.

4 Keep the child busy with activities that require movement. Ask the child to run an errand for you, to stack books, to sort papers, and so on.

5 Point out to the student that the practice has been noticed. Explain why masturbating in public is unacceptable.

6 Seek the help of the school nurse, counselor, or social worker who may be aware of the child's background. These professionals may have experience with strategies to help the student stop the practice in public.

MATURATIONAL DELAY

CAPSULE: All children do not develop and mature at the same pace; therefore all are not equally and automatically ready to do first-grade work at age six. Students who lag maturationally behind their peers experience difficulty in school. A delay in maturation becomes less of an issue in open or nongraded institutions.

In typically graded situations, students with maturational lags often do not fit in socially. They may engage in parallel play, as opposed to peer interaction. Academically, learning to read on a schedule with classmates may be challenging, if not impossible. Generally, holding a student back from entering school is preferable, in self-esteem terms, to the student's having to repeat a grade later. Teachers and parents should work together to determine readiness for school.

OPTIONS

1 Administer verbal and non-verbal school readiness tests, such as a kindergarten skills inventory, to all students. If a question exists regarding a child's readiness to enter school, request that the child be given psychological tests to add to the information available.

2 Assign the student with a maturational delay, who is already in the classroom, a "buddy" to assist with in-class work. Perhaps the assigned helper will also become a companion on the playground.

3 Give students with maturational lags opportunities to select their own best work

for display purposes. They can become active evaluators of their work, aware of their own maturing.

4 Refrain from labeling the child "immature." A negative label helps no one.

5 Study student artwork. Students with maturational delays will indicate less awareness of the world around them than more mature students display. Consult an art educator for help in understanding students' artwork.

MESSINESS

SEE ALSO
Littering

CAPSULE: Teachers and parents express a great deal of concern over the fact that their students or offspring are without a doubt among the messiest, untidiest children they've ever known. They voice the complaint, aware or not that the child may be using them as a model (or may be responding adversely to their fastidiousness).

Some students are so creative and lost in a world of ideas that they seem oblivious to any array of things around them, orderly or not. Some contribute to messiness as a direct result of their clumsiness or lack of motor control. Others who have always had someone picking up after them just don't know how to curtail messiness. Students enjoy a common-sense approach to orderliness as a means of getting their work done in a satisfactory manner.

OPTIONS

1 Agree upon a regular time to have cleanup sessions.

2 Develop a hierarchy of expectations that is pertinent to each child's problem. Begin with the simplest requirement, such as handing in uncrumpled papers with the student's name written clearly on them. Gradually increase the expectations.

3 Give the messy students important jobs that will make them more aware of orderliness. Some examples: checking desks for wastepaper; being in charge of collecting wastepaper; or sorting things.

4 Have the students share with the entire class some of their school labor-saving devices, ideas, or practices, such as zipper folders for certain kinds of papers, manila folders for others, colored tabs to denote papers in certain subjects, small boxes for clips and erasers, pencil cases, books stacked in the order that they are used during the day, and so on.

5 Keep corrections pertaining to messiness impersonal. (Instead of "Julie, you're a

messy girl!" say, "Julie, your desk could use organizing.")

6 Provide some times, places, and activities in which messiness is acceptable.

7 Reward obvious attempts to be more organized. Allow primary children to wear a special badge or bracelet indicating their good work; send a note home to the parent praising the child for efforts to be neater; telephone the parent and praise the child's efforts; reflect the student's efforts to improve by writing meaningful comments on his or her report card. Praise students directly to reinforce their attempts to be orderly.

8 State clearly what your position is with regard to order. ("So that everyone will have the best possible working conditions, I'm requesting that each of you keep your belongings in your [desk, locker, carton, shelf]. Any items I find on the floor or in my way I'll keep until Friday afternoon, which will be 'Reclamation Day.' That means that if you leave something out on Monday you will have to get along without it for a week.")

MULTICULTURAL POPULATION

SEE ALSO
Bilingual Children
Culturally Diverse

CAPSULE: Increasing numbers of children from other countries are enrolling in American schools. Students come from diverse cultural and socioeconomic backgrounds from all over the globe. Being in a strange land with an unfamiliar language can cause communication and learning problems. Learning the new language and finding a place to fit in are the keys to cultural adjustment and academic achievement.

OPTIONS

1 Become acquainted with the cultural values of new students. Develop an understanding of and a tolerance for values which may not be the same as those of the prevailing culture.

2 Encourage new students to share customs and stories of their native lands. Artifacts, clothing, and toys from other countries can be interesting and broadening to the class.

3 Investigate starting a "Limited English Proficiency" program, if the population warrants it. Teachers trained in ESL (English as a Second Language) curriculum and methodology can help students learn English quickly, within the context of academic instruction.

4 Investigate the availability of bilingual teachers, aides, or volunteers to ease translation and communication.

5 Learn some basic vocabulary of the languages spoken by the children. Although children should concentrate on learning English, hearing others attempt to communicate in the native language reinforces the significance of the language and enhances students' self-esteem.

NAME-SLURRING

SEE ALSO
Aggressiveness
Bullying
Fearfulness
Teasing

CAPSULE: Name-slurring is a form of aggression meant to hurt accosted students, to rob them of their dignity. Any aspect of an individual that can be perceived as different—his or her racial or ethnic background, wearing glasses or braces, or being heavy or skinny—can make the student a target. Slurs on a person's heritage and/or identity can have long-lasting, damaging effects. In order to stop or at least to control name-slurring, a teacher should work with both aggressors and victims to help students understand themselves and why slurs benefit no one.

OPTIONS

1 Assist recipients of name-slurring to deal with assaults to their egos. Give attacked students high-level, responsible classroom tasks, such as attendance taking or homework checking.

2 Call the slur-giver and the recipient together for a report of the experience. Ask the students for permission to videotape or make an audiotape of the conver-sation. Play back the tape for the students. A direct confrontation with their own words and behavior may be a sobering experience.

3 Discuss slurs in the class-room. Explain to students what causes name-calling and how negative effects can result for all involved. Ask students to volunteer sample strategies for deal-ings with slurs.

4 Meet one-on-one with the aggressor to elicit why that individual feels that "putting down" others is appropriate. Explain that using slurs is usually a signal that the initiator suffers from low self-esteem. Confer with the parents to plan esteem-building methods for the student.

NOISINESS

SEE ALSO
Attention Seeking
Talking Out

CAPSULE: Noisy students are accomplishing their goals which include making themselves heard and noticed. They like the clatter of pencils, the thump of feet, the banging of doors, and especially the sounds of their own voices. Assure these students that they do not have to be noisy to get your attention. Students can gain recognition if they behave in normal, acceptable ways.

OPTIONS

1 Allow for a student's noisy conduct, without censure, during certain times of the day. Expect no noise at other times.

2 Enlist the help of the entire class in designing a classroom arrangement that will keep the noise at a desirable level. Involvement in such a plan may tone down noisy students or make them aware of others' need for less noise.

3 Experiment with the best location in the room for the noisy one. Placement next to a quiet student may provide a good role model.

4 Signal the noisy student with a silent cue: blink the lights, write a message on the board, raise your hand, touch your lips, or hold your ears.

5 Speak in a near-whisper to the class. ("May I have your attention?") Repeat yourself until the message has gotten around to the noisy student. Stand in front of the room, silently, until all quiet down.

6 Stand at the door as the students enter the classroom. There you can casually remind the noisy one to "turn the volume down."

7 State, simply, what the situation is. "The group cannot work productively with this level of noise." Use peer pressure to help the noisy student control the volume level.

NONTALKERS

SEE ALSO
Withdrawn Children

CAPSULE: Occasionally, students in the primary grades will not talk for long periods of time, sometimes for as long as a year or more. It is tempting to conclude that something is drastically wrong, since most children love to chatter. However, the silent child may actually be adjusting to a new situation in a self-satisfying manner. The attention gleaned from solicitous classmates and teachers may, itself, be a reward, and the need to perform is often reduced to nil since the child has already been labeled "shy" or "frightened." What may have begun as fear of a new situation could easily have evolved into a most gratifying role. Telling the child that you know the game and that you don't like it is unlikely to bring a change. Likewise, the urge to "shake a child into talking" can be great, but prognosis for success thereby is highly questionable. Resist punitive action and exercise patience and fortitude with a consistent approach.

O P T I O N S

1 Be explicit and expectant when asking a child to do something. Resist temptation to plead, beg, or question. Instead, say, "Billy, tell us by drawing a picture of how Baby Bear felt when he found his chair was broken."

2 Become acquainted with the child's family and its history. (Were siblings nontalkers? Does the child talk at home? How do the parents discipline the child?)

3 Clue in the class about the reasons you work with the nontalker as you do. When the nontalker is absent, ask the students to refrain from speaking for the child or explaining the behavior with comments such as "He's shy," or "She can't talk." Try to explain that as long as they do that the nontalker won't talk, so as not to make liars out of them.

4 Consult the family doctor (with permission from the family, of course). You can learn from the doctor whether the silence stems from organic or psychological problems.

5 Consult a speech therapist.

6 Demonstrate warmth and affection for the child by occasional touching, hand holding, and patting.

7 Exhibit, without comment, the good work of the child.

8 Give the child many opportunities to draw or paint. The child can communicate using a pencil, crayon, or brush, if vocal communication doesn't exist.

9 Maintain anecdotal records of the child's conduct for clues to periods of stress, abandon, and unhappiness. Record precisely what the child does, not your interpretation of the behavior.

10 Offer a reward to the nontalker. Use a reward that you know is prized by the child. ("Chantal, when you are able to say 'good morning' to me, you may use my clipboard for a day.")

NOTE PASSING

CAPSULE: Note passing is a tantalizing student activity. Its secretive nature is mystifying and exciting. A juicy morsel of gossip makes student-to-student written communication even more exciting.

Good teaching allows little time for other than curriculum-based note writing. Most teachers are not bothered by occasional notes. There will, of course, be times when communications of any kind are taboo (during tests for example). A general understanding early in the semester regarding proper handling of note-writing incidents can be helpful.

OPTIONS

1 Ask the note writers to delay the practice. ("Tom, please do your math now and write your note after class.")

2 Discourage note passing by explaining that any notes passed during class will become your property.

3 Give opportunities for "writing to learn" activities, such as journal entries and note writing to the teacher.

NUTRITIONAL DEFICIENCIES

SEE ALSO
Allergies
Eating Disorders
Health Problems

CAPSULE: In order to maximize learning, students need to be healthy. The ways students think, feel, and perceive their environment are often affected by dietary intake. Teachers and parents should be alert to difficulties in concentrating or sudden weight changes as symptomatic of nutritional deficiencies.

OPTIONS

1 Become knowledgeable about nutrition through independent study. Attend workshops addressing nutrition and behavior.

2 Bring symptoms to parents' attention. Ask parents to refer the student to a physician.

3 Consult the school nurse or counselor for informative presentations on food and its impact on the ability to concentrate and learn.

4 Observe students' intake. If they are plying themselves with junk food and sweets, they may display symptoms of hyperactivity.

OBESITY

O

SEE ALSO
Dependency
Eating Disorders
Health Problems
Physical Differences
Self-Concept

CAPSULE: According to some authorities, approximately 20 percent of American high-school seniors are overweight. A weight problem is generally caused by a caloric intake that exceeds growth needs and energy expenditure. Through the school, professionals can impress upon all students the relationship between food intake and physical exercise. Ideally, every student, from kindergarten through twelfth grade, should participate in a well-planned health and physical education program, enhanced by units in nutrition.

Because obesity is generally physically unhealthy, as well as frequently detrimental to one's self-esteem, school personnel should help to empower students to lose weight. With parents and physicians, teachers can help obese students initiate programs for controlling weight. In educating students about health, teachers can explain that weight is basically controlled by three elements: genes (over which one has no control), eating habits (which have been cultivated by family and lifestyle), and exercise (over which one definitely has control). Teachers should inform students that dieting should take place under the supervision of a doctor and that crash diets are often risky and harmful.

O P T I O N S

1 Consult the physical education teacher about how to help the obese child enjoy losing weight. Advise the child to work directly with the physical education or health teacher for specific help with a nutrition and exercise program.

2 Examine the child's health record to learn whether there is a history of obesity, whether another disease or condition reflects itself in obesity, or whether the student is under a doctor's care.

3 Hold a conference with the child's parents or guardians.

Learn the dietary habits of the family. Recommend that the entire family work with the school nurse or their own physician.

4 Involve children with weight problems in physical activities commensurate with their ability to perform without humiliation. Allowing them to sit on the sidelines is a disservice to them. Plan gradual induction into increased physical activity.

5 Observe whether the child eats compulsively during times of stress. Refer such problems to a counselor.

OBSCENITIES

SEE ALSO
Attention Seeking
Rudeness

C A P S U L E : Syndicated newspaper columnist Bob Greene once described obscenity as the "curse of the casual age." Long regarded by those in the "establishment" as the language of anger and ugliness, obscenities are creeping into casual conversations at all societal levels. Language models in the media, especially movies, are increasingly uncensored and obscene. As part of a well-rounded education, teachers should emphasize that although students may be routinely exposed to obscene language elsewhere, this language has no place in the safe environment of the classroom.

O P T I O N S

1 Discuss the use of obscene language with parents. Work with parents to reinforce the notion of appropriate language in certain situations.

2 Hold class discussions on: Why do some people choose to use obscene language? How do obscenities become part of acceptable language, or do they? Is using obscene language "ok" in some places, when in other places obscenities are totally out of place? Adjust the level of questions to the age group.

3 Insist that obscenities are not to be spoken (or yelled) in school or on the play-ground. Establish consequences for the use of obscene language, such as after-school "enrichment" sessions in which students and teacher discuss the significance of language as symbols to communicate meaning.

4 Praise students for "cleaning up their acts." "I'm proud of the positive way you have been communicating lately."

5 Remind students that school is not the place for obscene language. Language that assaults anyone's senses is inappropriate for a "socializing" institution.

OVERACHIEVERS

SEE ALSO
Burnout
Grades
Sibling Rivalry
Stress
Underachievers

CAPSULE: Overachievers can be described as students who are so highly motivated that they put their efforts into "overdrive" in order to accomplish goals. Students who demonstrate a pattern of over-achievement may lack a well-balanced life and the ability to relax and enjoy their accomplishments. Some teachers describe overachievers as those who are motivated for the wrong reasons. For example, because of fear of parental disapproval and rejection, students may relentlessly pursue impossibly high goals determined by parents. Overachievers may be compensating for low self-esteem with an unusually strong drive for personal recognition. Some overachievers can keep up a consistent level of performance; others slump into depression and substandard performance when the adrenaline runs dry.

OPTIONS

1 Celebrate small accomplishments. Break down large tasks into small components to help students experience success with attainable goals.

2 Conduct a class discussion (see Appendix) on intrinsic and extrinsic rewards. Ask students to provide examples of each type of reward and of the feelings involved when working for rewards.

3 Discuss the stress-ridden overachiever with parents and the school counselor. Help the student set realistic goals and monitor progress.

4 Observe closely the grade-obsessed student who responds with tears and blaming when receiving any grade other than an "A." Communicate with parents regarding de-emphasizing external pressures and expectations.

PARANOIA

SEE ALSO
Health Problems

CAPSULE: Paranoia describes a system of defenses associated with feelings of persecution, excessive distrust of others, and irrational suspiciousness.

Teachers may be able to recognize characteristics of paranoia, but they should not label a child "paranoid," even though the label might be quite accurate. Diagnosing paranoia is the business of qualified health professionals. Students who express paranoiac tendencies need help in facing reality and in coping with life on a day-to-day basis. Teachers are in a key position to help relieve the student of some anxieties.

OPTIONS

1 Allow students to talk freely about their persecutions. Practice active listening and repeat students' comments back to them. Respond in declarative sentences. ("You feel that Sue thinks you're not doing a good job as committee chairperson.")

2 Help the students who feel that "everybody's picking on them" identify *exactly* what gives them that feeling. If they persist in clinging to a false premise, they may indeed be paranoid and in need of professional treatment.

3 Refer such students to the nurse or social worker at school.

PASSIVE BEHAVIOR

SEE ALSO
Attention Seeking
Fearfulness

CAPSULE: Unlike the aggressive person, the passive individual fails to express feelings, needs, and affections to others. Anything that is felt is put on hold, for fear dominates and takes control of behavior. People who behave passively tend to let others take advantage of them. They may feel uncomfortable, but they're unsure of any avenues to freedom, so they bottle up their feelings and surprise even themselves with an occasional, sudden explosion of pent-up sentiment.

When people behave passively they may harbor unexpressed feelings of anger, tension, or anxiety. Since they don't stand up for their rights, they are prime targets for being pushed around by others. Passive behavior in one permits aggressive behavior in another. Still another result of passive behavior in a student is the encouragement of passive conduct in another student, especially for those who already have a tendency toward submissive behavior.

Control is often a major factor in this kind of responsiveness. When passive behavior is used to control another it becomes what is known as "passive-aggressiveness" or "passive resistance." Acts of quiet noncooperation or the well-known "silent treatment" can be maddening since misunderstandings are inevitable when people do not communicate directly.

O P T I O N S

1 Arrange to teach or have taught by another member of your faculty some lessons in assertive behavior, which allow both parties to relate to each other on an equal footing. When the students realize that they can say *no* and *yes* without feeling guilty or embarrassed you will know you've made progress.

2 Encourage passive students to practice making honest declarative statements to aggressive classmates when confronted. Role play (see Appendix) conflict situations in class.

3 Pair a passive student with a more outgoing one for certain activities. (See Buddy System, Appendix.)

PHYSICAL DIFFERENCES

SEE ALSO
Health Problems
Self-Concept

C A P S U L E : One's physical characteristics affect self-concept from birth to death. Many of the problems that develop in school are related to students' perceptions about their physical differences. Any unusual characteristics can make a youngster feel self-conscious and can affect behavior.

Some students enter school with physique problems that hold little or no promise of change—the malformed, the paraplegic, the burn-scarred. The vast majority have fleeting worries regarding their bodies. During preadolescence, when internal rumblings begin, even so-called normal children harbor feelings of inadequacy. The "early developing" girl and "late blooming" boy may feel conspicuous and out of place.

Question whether the "too tall" child slumps to be more like the others, or whether the "too fat" child is sedentary just to avoid being teased. These students need positive reinforcement of their obviously excellent qualities and minimal attention to their differentness.

Your attitude toward marked physical differences can provide the impetus for general acceptance of the exceptional student in your class.

O P T I O N S

1 Be sure the classroom furniture is comfortable for the student. Chairs and tables that are too high or too low can precipitate negative behavior.

2 Consult the student's parents to learn how they feel and how you can work together on the problem.

3 Cultivate a spirit of accepting people's physical differences. One way to do this is to play the game "Affirmation." In this game, each student states his or her name, mentions a physical characteristic he or she has, and explains an advantage of having this particular characteristic. For example,

the first student might say, "I'm Joe. I'm tall. Because I'm tall I can tip the basketball into the hoop easily." The next player might say, "I'm Flo. I'm tiny. Because I'm tiny I can hide under the teacher's desk." The game continues in this manner until all the students have affirmed themselves in some way.

4 Provide the students with a variety of published materials dealing with the different body types (endomorph, mesomorph, ectomorph) and the variability of chronological age in reaching puberty.

5 Refer the student to the school counselor or to medical personnel.

6 Share stories of people whose unusual physical characteristics were determining factors in saving a situation or whose physical limitations did not deter notable achievements. (See Bibliotherapy, Appendix.)

PORNOGRAPHY

CAPSULE: Pornography is more than harmless dirty pictures; it can contain material that displays sado-masochistic behavior with a special emphasis on degrading women and children. Whether pornographic material is hard core (showing explicit sexual acts or acts of pain or humiliation) or soft core (trade magazines), its presence in the classroom will detract from students' engagement in the learning process. Without creating excessive commotion, which adds to the illicit excitement of the pornographic material, the teacher should get rid of it in a matter-of-fact, efficient manner.

OPTIONS

1 Inform parents if hard-core material is being distributed or if the problem recurs. Parents should be aware of unusual reading (or perhaps selling) habits.

2 Keep pornographic material. Share it with school or local authorities.

3 Tell students directly that pornography has no place in the classroom. Explain to students why pornography is inappropriate and insist that they abide by your rules.

PREJUDICE

SEE ALSO
Bilingual Children
Multicultural Population

CAPSULE: Over three decades ago, Oscar Hammerstein II wrote a lyric for the musical *South Pacific* about how people acquire prejudices: "You've got to be carefully taught." Students appear at school with prejudices already ingrained, having been "carefully taught" by a variety of sources. Sometimes these prejudices manifest themselves in acts of cruelty.

To counteract the effects of prejudice, the classroom is an excellent place to teach tolerance and acceptance. Through education, students can become aware of the resurgence of "hate groups," both in our country and internationally. Students also can learn how acts of prejudice can lead to devastating consequences.

OPTIONS

1 Celebrate multicultural diversity in the classroom. Emphasize positive contributions of varied racial and ethnic groups.

2 Explore how prejudice can lead to human horrors. Discuss current events related to acts of prejudice as well as historical events connected to prejudice.

3 Incorporate available educational materials other than textbooks to teach the importance of tolerance and the effects of discrimination and resentment. Seminars or mini-courses such as "Facing History and Our-selves"—a Holocaust study package—serve to instruct teachers about how they can make students aware of propaganda techniques and how to discriminate between right and wrong.

PRE-VACATION SYNDROME

SEE ALSO
Hyperactivity

CAPSULE: Pre-vacation syndrome is characterized by a rash of absences a few days before a scheduled holiday. Parents contribute to the problem when they view getting a jump on vacation as more important than the business of school. Occasionally, family plans absolutely necessitate early departures. In those cases, teacher, student, and parent can create a fair arrangement, so that the student is not penalized for something beyond control.

Teachers often dread the frenetic atmosphere in school before holidays. However, careful planning combined with a jovial and no-nonsense attitude can make the prevacation days productive and enjoyable.

OPTIONS

1 Ask the students to help plan assignments for the period before the holiday. ("Pre-vacation days are often wasted because the holiday atmosphere and the school-work seem to work against each other, so let's make a 'then' plan, now.")

2 Plan activities that contribute to a happy mood without overstimulating the students.

Some examples include spelling bees or trivia games based on course content.

3 Plan and implement meaningful learning activities which last until the last minute before vacation. Give parents *no excuse* to take children out of school early because "All they do is have parties or play games, anyway."

PROCRASTINATION

SEE ALSO
Anxiety
Homework
Self-Concept
Study Skills

CAPSULE: Procrastinators are difficult to deal with because of the unkept promise that they "will do it later." Almost everybody puts off completing tasks that are dull, unpleasant, or difficult. However, habitual procrastinators may have a poor concept of time, and as long as nothing cataclysmic happens, they float along. When something that really matters occurs, respect for time and energy spurts noticeably. Homework is often the source of frustrating efforts on the part of parents to teach children to budget time and avoid delays in completing work.

Studies indicate that many students procrastinate because they are afraid of failure, have low self-esteem, are perfectionists, lack study skills, or are rebelling against authority. Whatever the reason, positive change can begin with conscientious redirection and clear goal setting. The teacher and parent can assist the student by holding to "one goal at a time." The satisfaction derived from completion of a job will carry the intrinsic bonus of raised self-esteem, better grades, and less concern with failure.

O P T I O N S

1 Help procrastinating students to structure jobs so that they take care of tasks on a schedule instead of trying to do them all at once. (What is best done right after school? Before dinner? On Monday? On Sunday afternoon?)

2 Refrain from bailing students out of situations that arise from procrastination. Bailing students out can enable them to continue the behavior. Why should students complete assignments on time if they receive the same credit for either timely or late completion?

3 Reward early or timely completion of tasks. ("You may do _____ after you have finished _____.")

READING PROBLEMS

SEE ALSO
Disabilities, Learning
Study Skills

CAPSULE: Poor reading limits students' progress in almost every educational area. Reading problems may stem from other problems, such as learning disabilities. Young students who encounter a great deal of difficulty while learning to read should be screened for learning disabilities. While learning disabilities, such as dyslexia (in which letters and numbers are perceived backwards, sometimes as mirror images) cannot be cured, with practice students can learn coping/compensating techniques.

In the current view of reading instruction, teachers should emphasize the active role readers play in interacting with text in order to create meaning. To help students relate to what is on the printed page, teachers should activate students' prior knowledge of subject matter. Once students find an aspect of the text which is related to prior experience, they can more easily comprehend new material.

OPTIONS

1 Awaken student interest in reading assignments. Conduct prereading exercises in which students make predictions about what will happen in text material. Sometimes a title or the first paragraphs of a book will give enough substance to engage students' curiosity. "What do you think will happen here? What do you think will be the main point of this reading?"

2 Engage students in writing about what they are reading. Connecting writing to reading can aid comprehension. In addition to responding to reading in prose form, students can construct outlines or maps (nonsequential diagrams) to represent information in visual form.

3 Provide instruction in specific reading strategies. For example, students can be taught to underline important words or phrases, to annotate their books, and to summarize regularly. In order to augment reading comprehension, students might read with pencils in their hands!

4 Talk about what has been read, one-to-one or in small groups. Often this "talk aloud" strategy with reciprocal questioning will help students to understand fine points, as well as general meaning, of the text.

5 Teach students the significance of textbook organization. Many texts have chapters and subchapters, with words or phrases in boldface print. Becoming aware of the special features of the text can help students to understand the patterns of text material.

REJECTED CHILDREN

SEE ALSO
Loneliness
Self-Concept
Sibling Rivalry

CAPSULE: Rejected children feel unpopular, unwanted, and unloved. Intense rejection affects mental health and the ability to cope with the demands of schoolwork. For this reason, teachers should become aware of the rejected child, not only for the sake of the individual but also for the sake of the group. (Research indicates that the presence of a severely rejected member does, indeed, make the group suffer.)

Children are often rejected by immature parents who, not having grown up themselves, don't want to be bothered with the rigors of child rearing. Consequently, they fail to take time to care for and train their children properly. Children feel that they are burdensome to adults. In addition to the weight of the school program, they carry unnecessary emotional burdens.

Some children are so threatened by the possibility of being abandoned that they are consumed with worry and therefore cannot function in school. Others are plagued with a need to be popular, and when rejected by a peer group they feel that their whole world has collapsed. To them, being rebuffed by their peers may be more devastating than parental disownership. Rejected children need assurances of security.

O P T I O N S

1 Ask rejected children to do something important for you. Help them overcome feelings of rejection by showing them that they are needed. ("Jo, could you help record absences in my gradebook?")

2 Assign an older student "mentor" to the rejected child. Identifying with someone older can often give the child feelings of security and status. (See Peer Mentors, Appendix.)

3 Assure all children through your consistent friendly conduct that you do not reject them—that you like them for special reasons. Become aware, through active listening, of the possible reasons why children feel rejected. Do they feel that you, the teacher, really accept them? Do their peers have a good reason for rejecting them?

4 Confer with the parents and the child. You may, on the basis of your conference, want to recommend that the school psychologist be consulted.

5 Keep anecdotal records of the child's behavior. These are notes regarding significant behaviors (both negative and exemplary), but without value judgment or interpretation, at least for the time being. Invite the school counselor to observe the child in the classroom. Discuss behaviors and help options with the counselor.

6 Set up friendly, small-group situations that have maximum chances of success. In planning a class party, for example, the rejected child can be responsible for contributing something that will be appreciated and enjoyed by the entire group and will warrant recognition.

RESTLESSNESS

SEE ALSO
Anxiety
Wanderers

CAPSULE: Some students have a difficult time sitting still for an entire lesson. For the student who is bored, unsure, or just "seatsick," the washroom can be a plausible retreat. Getting permission to go to the washroom is the ticket down the hallway to visit someplace or someone else.

Although elimination should be treated matter-of-factly, the teacher should make sure to avoid excessive wandering. Generally, a policy of not leaving the classroom, except in unusual or emergency situations, is effective. The teacher should encourage individuals who have special needs to discuss them privately so that accommodations can be made.

OPTIONS

1 Begin class activities promptly. Generate so much interest that the students won't want to leave, and continue activities until the bell rings.

2 Check discreetly whether restlessness has exceptional physical causes. If necessary, discuss the restless behavior with the parents.

3 Discuss with your students, during your class organization the first week of school, how you will handle "basic needs" problems. Peer pressure will then help to govern the students' use or abuse of any privilege.

4 Refer restless students to medical personnel.

5 Use a sign-out sheet, allowing only one student out of a classroom at a time.

6 Use a wooden pass that carries the number of the room or the name of the student's teacher. Possession of the pass indicates that the child has permission to go to the washroom or through the halls.

7 Vary classroom activities so that resltess students have opportunities for physical mobility without having to leave the classroom.

RUDENESS

CAPSULE: Rudeness is the result of bad training, anger, or both. With a good model, most students pick up polite behavior. If the climate in your classroom is a healthy one, little need be said about good manners.

School cafeterias are sometimes bastions of wild behavior and crudity expressed by elbowing one's way to a destination; bolting, throwing, and tossing food disdainfully into the trash can; or yelling and whistling. Is it any wonder school administrators often opt to hire outsiders to come in and "police" cafeterias? The following suggestions may help redirect rude behaviors into polite ones.

OPTIONS

1 Establish with the students norms of conduct for the class. They may elect to identify offensive behaviors and the attendant consequences. (See Organizing a Classroom, Appendix.)

2 Practice polite behavior as an integral part of homeroom or of a regular class. ("Tomorrow we'll practice introducing strangers to each other. Shaking hands properly is an art.")

3 Reinforce, casually, students' natural acts of politeness. ("Barbara, thank you for offering Mrs. T. your seat when she entered the room.")

4 Role play (see Appendix) a glaring incident of bad manners. ("This is the situation. The class has invited parents to watch a play and have refreshments. Ron dashes in front of an adult and grabs three cookies, nearly tripping the adult.") Discuss the effects of one's bad manners on others.

5 Take the impolite student aside for a talk about rudeness. First, assess whether or not the student was fully aware of the indiscretion. Ask *what* was done (not *why*) and assume for the time being that the description of the conduct is a deterrent in itself.

RUNAWAYS

SEE ALSO
Dropouts, Potential
Stress

CAPSULE: Runaways are young people who leave home for at least one night without permission from a parent or guardian. Some children, often referred to as "throwaways," are forced out of their homes by the adults in charge. In 1989, the United States Department of Health and Human Services estimated that there are approximately 1.1 million runaways and homeless youths each year.

Teenagers run away because they face what they perceive to be irresolvable conflicts at home. Conflicts may stem from communication problems, unrealistic expectations, or more commonly, some form of abuse. Most runaways stay in the county or metropolitan area in which they live, and most return home within a week. For those who return home, families should focus on issues that caused the child to run away. Young people who do not return home may live on the street, where they may fall prey to pimps or drug dealers.

OPTIONS

1 Contact the National Runaway Switchboard (1-800-621-4000) if you know of someone who has run away. Switchboard workers can provide the names and phone numbers of the nearest shelters where young people may seek refuge.

2 Help returning students to re-enter school. Be available to talk and to listen to students' concerns. Give generously of time and attention to help students make up schoolwork.

3 Keep a well-defined attendance reporting procedure. If a student is absent from school without written or verbal parental authorization, contact parents immediately. The phone call from someone at school may be the first clue to the parents that the child is missing.

4 Listen for signs of distress or for students' threats about running away. If a student seems to be serious about leaving home, refer that individual to the school psychologist or social worker. A school professional or other counselor can work with the family to alleviate stressors on the child. They can also work toward reunifying the family.

School Phobia

SEE ALSO
Anxiety
Fearfulness

CAPSULE: A phobia is an abnormal fear related to a specific situation. People who experience excessive fear may be quite aware that their phobias are unreasonable, even foolish, but they are unable to change their feelings. Many psychologists feel that phobias are born of early childhood experiences associated with shame or embarrassment.

Students who experience school phobia may feel that school is a hostile environment. A happy, normal setting provides the best therapy. Establish a warm, nurturing climate in the classroom. Be low-keyed about seating, pairing students, and changes in tempo of instruction—all of which can be upsetting to the phobic child. The school counselor can be extremely helpful in planning approaches to be used.

OPTIONS

1 Be nondirective when you and the phobic student discuss fear of coming to school. ("You sometimes feel as though you'd rather play sick and stay home than come to school.") Abstain from censoring the responses.

2 Develop a hierarchy of fear-ridden steps and lead the child toward being comfortable with them. This is sometimes called "desensitization" and may involve from five to twenty steps, depending upon the case. An effective method of desensitization is to help the student prepare a list of steps to take to overcome the fear. One such list might start like this:

1. Get books ready to take to school tomorrow.

2. Get clothes ready for tomorrow.

3. [*next morning*] Get dressed for school.

4. Walk with sister to bus.

5. Get on bus and ride to school.

The list would continue in a similar fashion until the student makes it to the classroom.

3 Hold a meeting of teachers, counselors, administrators, and parents to gather information and plan appropriate strategy. With a phobic child, consistency is of utmost importance. (See Staff Meeting, Appendix.)

4 Use extrinsic rewards (see Appendix) to encourage the child to attend school. Personalize the student's education for gradual induction into academic pursuits so that the student sees purpose and joy in school.

SELF-CONCEPT

SEE ALSO
Ashamed Students
Underachievers

CAPSULE: Simply stated, a person's self-concept is a deep-down, personal view of self. It is a privately viewed self-portrait—a measure of one's self-esteem. Idealistic parents and teachers want children to begin with, and continue through school with, a view of themselves that, like fine wine, improves with age. Too often this dream is dashed—for clear, but indefensible, reasons.

Children's self-portraits are painted by others. They are the products of innumerable people who, in one way or another, brush their lives and tell them what they're worth. Adding up the pluses and minuses, children develop something called a "self-concept," good or poor. Reckless and defensive judging, evaluating, and criticizing may take from children the ability to evaluate themselves.

Many responses that contribute to a poor self-concept are proffered in ignorance. The "good-bad" dichotomy is a classic example. Children who are constantly told they are "good" would like to know why, and children who are told they are "bad" would also like explicitness. In using adjectives and adverbs, teachers should focus on behavior or work, not on the students themselves.

O P T I O N S

1 Converse often, and informally, with students away
from the classroom setting.
Note their expressions of
anxiety, defensiveness, and
hope. Don't forget to let
them know that you feel
they are worthwhile and
important.

2 Help students identify what
they would like to be able
to accomplish, then give
them step-by-step assistance
in attaining their goals. (See
Flight Plan, Appendix.)

3 Permit students to do something special for an individual or for a class other than

their own. ("Tina, would
you read your story to Mr.
Z's class?") Permit them to
show their good work to
someone they admire
(nurse, principal, counselor,
custodian).

4 Praise students' classwork
with specifics, not generali-
ties. ("Your poem is both
moving and melodic. The
meter is perfect in all but
the two last lines—or did
you purposely decide to end
it that way?") Compare such
a statement with, "Great
poem!" or "I didn't think you
could write so well.")

SEXUAL ASSAULT

SEE ALSO
Abused Children, Sexually
AIDS
Exhibitionism
Health Problems
Masturbation

C A P S U L E : Sexual assault refers to sexual contact without consent. It includes any unwanted touching or
fondling of genitals or breasts and forced penetration
(rape). According to recent reports, approximately 20
percent of sexual assaults are committed by strangers;
therefore, 80 percent of forced sexual encounters occur
between people who know each other. The terms
"acquaintance rape" and more popularly "date rape"
have been coined for sexual assaults that result in

penetration occurring between two people who know each other.

Most rapes occur, with the male as the aggressor, against women aged fifteen to twenty-four. However, a large number of middle-school students and males are also sexual assault victims. Students should be taught that forced, unwanted sexual contact is a violent crime; it is not an act of affection. Everyone has the right to say "no," and "no" means "NO!" Students should also know that sexual assault is not the fault of the victim; the sole fault lies with the aggressor.

OPTIONS

1 Explain helpful procedures for sexual assault victims. Patient listening by friends and professional counseling can help victims through the trauma. Rape victims should be examined medically as soon as possible after the rape. Although the normal desire is to cleanse oneself after a rape, the victim should not shower before being examined. Semen and other samples may prove useful later in criminal prosecution.

2 Give students concrete information about how to minimize the chances of sexual assault. For example, young people might double-date or go out as part of a group, especially on a first date.

They might also avoid isolated areas where dangerous situations could arise.

3 Help students to identify behaviors that make them uneasy or afraid and to set limits. Young people need to know that they have the right not to be talked to or touched in inappropriate ways. They can convey their feelings with strong statements and body language— no apologies or excuses are necessary.

4 Plan and implement a sexual assault prevention program. The program might contain (but not be limited to) information about sexual harassment and acquaintance rape, an explanation of effective

verbal and nonverbal communication in personal relationships, physical self-defense training, information regarding the relationship of alcohol use to sexual assault, and a sensitivity training segment for boys.

5 Use role playing (see Appendix) to create scenarios in which an individual could be susceptible to sexual attack. Through watching and analyzing classroom skits, students can begin to recognize situations in which an unwelcome encounter could occur.

SEXUALLY TRANSMITTED DISEASES (STDS)

SEE ALSO
AIDS

CAPSULE: Over twenty-five forms of STDs have been identified and are spreading at an epidemic rate. Diseases range from the most dangerous (AIDS, which is deadly) to others that can be treated with antibiotics. Some of the more common STDs include chlamydia, herpes, genital warts, gonorrhea, syphilis, and varied types of vaginitis. Symptoms may include discharge, burning, itching, and sores and growths in the genital area. Abdominal pain in women can be a symptom of PID (pelvic inflammatory disease), a complication of chlamydia, gonorrhea, or other infections. Because some symptoms take months, even years, to appear, the partner of an infected individual must seek medical care.

Whether or not young people in school are currently sexually active, they are at risk. Studies indicate that most young people become sexually active either while they are still in school or shortly after they leave school. The best form of treatment is prevention. Students must become educated about STDs so that they know how to prevent and deal with them.

OPTIONS

1 Encourage students to seek early treatment. Both a potentially infected individual and that person's partner should see a doctor or visit a clinic.

2 Implement a sex education unit or course, possibly within the physical education, health, or science curriculum. The course should be taught matter-of-factly and should include the scope of the STD problem, symptoms, and methods of prevention, control, and cure.

3 Tell students about the VD National Hotline (1-800-227-8922; in California 1-800-982-5883). Generally, the hotlines are open 8 a.m. to 8 p.m. weekdays and can provide information about where and how to get treatment.

Sibling Rivalry

SEE ALSO
Jealousy
Twins

CAPSULE: The term "sibling rivalry" immediately implies the need for family involvement and cooperation. Depending upon children's freedom to express themselves within their family, rivalry will be expressed in a variety of ways, ranging from excessive competitiveness to almost complete withdrawal. Wherever there are two or more people, competitiveness may become unhealthy. Knowing this, the astute adult capitalizes on opportunities to clarify with children the fact that a person's uniqueness is dependent upon differences and that whether differences *divide* or *unite* is entirely up to us. Parents and teacher need to remind themselves to suppress temptations to (1) compare a slow child with a fast-learning sibling, (2) to discuss the children's inequities in public, (3) to direct overcompensatory behavior toward the lesser-skilled, thereby creating dependency, or (4) to express disappointment, either verbally or through body language.

The school and the family should work together on sibling-rivalry problems because unresolved hostility in the early years may find dramatic expression in adulthood. Open, honest acceptance of all children for what they are is preferred to a slavish attempt to "treat all children exactly alike," regardless of how ridiculous that can get. Sooner or later children learn that different age groups, people with certain competencies, and others receive certain benefits. Show all children that you accept them and that what they are is good enough to please you.

OPTIONS

1 Compliment children on things they can do well and avoid references to their siblings.

2 Encourage siblings to pursue different areas of interest. Instead of watching brothers vie with one another in sports, for example, encourage one of them to participate in a different field.

3 Pair the jealous sibling with one whose needs are dissimilar and who may become a model for the child.

4 Reward *both* siblings for abstaining from overt rivalry. ("Look, girls, half the time I'm not sure who's responsible for the squabbles, so let's just say that if you can settle your own differences for the next four hours there'll be a surprise for both of you." *Note:* Failure to come through would be unforgivable!)

5 Talk frankly about the privileges different age groups can expect. ("When you're Tom's age you, too, will be permitted to _____.")

6 Use nondirective statements to clarify the student's feelings about a sibling. ("You feel that your sister gets more attention than you do.") Allow the student to discuss feelings about the sibling with your participation as active, empathetic listener.

SLAM BOOKS

CAPSULE: Students on the junior-high and high-school levels often engage in "slam book" or "truth book" use, through which they express their preferences or hatreds for others. In slam books, a student's name usually appears at the top of each page, and below it statements or expressions about that student are written, the writers being identified by numbers only. (The key is usually in the front of the notebook, so it's easy to check the identification of any particular writer). The students who instigate the movement are usually among the very vocal and critical. They are often cruel in their remarks about classmates. (Teachers are not spared, either.) Sensitive students who take these evaluations of their classmates to heart are often deeply hurt. Occasionally you can wait this one out, realizing that "this, too, will pass," but the following actions may be appropriate.

OPTIONS

1 Confiscate the slam book if it interferes with the class proceedings. ("I'm sorry, Lou, but I find it very hard to keep my mind on the lesson when that slam book is floating around. I'll keep it for you until the end of the period.") Put it in a drawer and give it to the student at the end of the period with the understanding that it won't show up again.

2 Create a journal assignment in which students must write positive comments about fellow class members. Give students practice in affirming their peers.

3 Discourage the circulation of slam books because of the hurt feelings they generate. Conduct a class discussion (see Appendix) about why they are inappropriate and damaging.

SLOW LEARNERS

SEE ALSO
Disabilities, Learning
Self-Concept

CAPSULE: In education circles, "slow learner" is ordinarily used to describe one in the seventy to eighty-five IQ bracket. Beware, however, of labeling a child "slow," particularly on the basis of only samples of behavior, such as standardized IQ tests. Teachers know that many students classified as "slow" have poor self-concepts. Teachers need to show persistence, high expectations, and genuine pleasure in helping students to achieve. Slow learners need an atmosphere of security, but this doesn't mean they need monotony. They need varied activities to keep them active and engaged in learning.

O P T I O N S

1 Arrange for the administration of untimed tests, since schoolwide standardized tests are not only invalid for slow learning children, but are also shattering to the egos of these students and their parents.

2 Discover the talents of the slow learners and build their egos by going as a class or a small group to see them perform. ("Sally is participating in the roller-skating derby next week. We could arrange to go and root for her.")

3 Enable slow learners to feel that they have some control over the learning situation. ("What shall we do first today, the numbers, the story, or the blends?")

4 Encourage students' excellence in something beyond the three Rs, such as athletic or musical activity. Incorporate references to these abilities when dealing with math and reading skills so that students feel proud for a real reason.

5 Establish a program that has short academic components and carries the lure of an appropriate reward for completion.

6 Get into the habit of calling attention to work that is well done, instead of to mistakes. Limit negative comments on students' papers. Avoid "bleeding" with the red pen.

7 Give slow learners opportunities to tutor younger children or to accompany them as helpers on a field trip. The increase in self-esteem should more than compensate for lost classroom time.

8 Keep in contact with parents regarding positive gains. ("Mrs. Greer, I just had to call you to tell you that Nancy has completed her _____ and now she's ready for _____.") After parents have been retrained to receive positive messages from the school, they are better able to absorb the occasional negative ones!

9 Praise students within earshot of their classmates. Like anybody else, they like others to hear good things said about them.

10 Use manipulative material to clarify concepts for the slow learners, particularly in math and science. Use right-brain hemisphere learning strategies, such as visual, spatial, and tactile techniques. (See Learning Styles, Appendix.)

SMOKING

CAPSULE: By now just about everyone in the United States must be aware of the Surgeon General's warning: "Smoking is dangerous to our health." Not only does smoking affect the smoker adversely, but it affects others through secondhand and sidestream smoke. Secondhand smoke is exhaled into the air by the smoker and then is inhaled by others in the vicinity. Sidestream smoke comes from the burning cigarette itself.

Young people often begin smoking as a way to gain social acceptance in some peer groups. They may enjoy nicotine's stimulant action and may feel slightly "high" from smoking. However, because nicotine is one of the most severely addictive drugs, students may become addicted to smoking, and quitting becomes difficult. Dealing with smoking in schools is easier now than it was years ago because the issues are fairly well defined.

O P T I O N S

1 Make the school a "smoke-free, tobacco-free" environment. No one should smoke on the premises, including adult school personnel. In a smoke-free environment, adults cannot provide negative role models for students who are thinking about smoking.

2 Provide information about smoking as part of the curriculum, perhaps in physical education, health, or science classes. Show students statistics and examples (especially visuals) about how smoking can adversely affect their health and their lives. Guest speakers who have suffered smoking-related cancer may also provide powerful messages.

3 Refer students who smoke to the counselor, the school nurse, or the student assistance counselor (who deals specifically with substance abuse) if the school has one. These qualified professionals can help students break the habit.

SOILING

SEE ALSO
Anxiety

C A P S U L E : Soiling usually occurs among the very young, though occasionally older students have "accidents" during times of excitement or fear. It is humiliating for all concerned, and the best approach is a matter-of-fact one—take care of the situation as quickly and as tactfully as possible. Soiling can mean several things: organic problems; open rebellion against parents, teachers, or other people; or a case of unexpected diarrhea. Avoid embarrassing students by asking why they did it (they don't know) or scolding them. Handle the matter in a low-key manner. They need to feel that you like and accept them, especially at a time like this. The following ideas may be useful.

OPTIONS

1 Allow students who have elimination problems to go to the washroom at any time, by request. In lower grades, they should not have to wait until the entire class visits the lavatory. In high school, they should not be forced to wait until the few minutes between classes.

2 Appraise the students' art work—it could give you a clue to their anxiety. If you're not professionally trained to do this, seek help.

3 Be alert to clues in the students' conversations that will indicate concerns or hostilities they may have. Share any clues with the doctor.

4 Change the class activity at the moment of crisis. Send the other students out to play, for example, while you attend to the matter.

5 Consult medical personnel and the school counselor.

SPEECH PROBLEMS

SEE ALSO
Stuttering

CAPSULE: Speech problems are usually the result of either physical impairment or poor speech models. In the case of impairment, specialists will be able to check causes and cures; in the case of poor models, retraining is necessary, and here parents and teachers must work together to provide good models. Early identification of speech problems can be the "ounce of prevention." In addition to using the skilled services of trained professionals, these practices may be helpful.

OPTIONS

1 Avoid mentioning the speech problem before a large group. Ask students when they would like some help and arrange to assist them privately.

2 Refer the student to a speech therapist for diagnosis and treatment if a therapist is available in the school. If no therapist is available, you might refer the student for outside help.

3 Send a note to the student's parents, mentioning the improved speech.

4 Surprise the student with a compliment about the improved speech. In addition to oral praise, you might write a note.

5 Use commercially programmed materials to handle increasingly complex speech and language patterns. A curriculum specialist or speech therapist might help gain access to materials.

6 Use extrinsic rewards (see Appendix) to reinforce a correct speech pattern that is gradually increased. In treating a student with a lisp, for example, you might begin by saying, "Jane, repeat after me: 'This is Susan.'" Next, increase to "This is Susan's sister." Finally, increase it to "These scissors are Susan's sister's." After each correct statement, reward the student. Make no comment after an incorrect version. *Caution:* Be alert to the temptation to overwork an exercise. Stop when the student feels successful and is not yet tired.

STEALING

SEE ALSO
Immoral Behavior
Lying

CAPSULE: Stealing can be exciting, and children who steal may never understand fully the psychologist's assertion that those who steal have poor self-images, are asking for love, are seeking attention, or are trying to get even with someone. To assert is easy; to effect change is not so easy. The adults who are faced with helping the student who steals must ask: Is this already a pattern of behavior or is it the first time the student has stolen? Is stealing condoned in the child's family? Is the student stealing to gain status with peers? Is the child stealing to gratify an immediate need (such as hunger), not having lived long enough to internalize the meaning of property rights?

Resist the temptation to preach or to scold a student publicly. Rather, concentrate on providing opportunities for the offending student to comprehend that every act brings its own consequences. Once restitution is made, assure the student through actions and words that the mistake is forgiven. The long road toward elimination of stealing begins with two words: "trust" and "respect."

O P T I O N S

1 Clarify the meaning of "ownership" and implant cultural attitudes through classroom activities. ("This is Jeff's book from his family's library and it is a very special volume—a first edition. We appreciate being able to look at it, and I know I can count on all of you to treat it with respect. You will note that there are several rare coins and feathers attached to the inside of the back cover." At this point you can elicit cautions to be taken when looking at Jeff's book.)

2 Elicit suggestions from the offender and then establish a fair payment for the offense, giving preference to work and time over money.

3 Expect common classroom supplies (scissors, pencils, chalk) to be returned to their proper places and let your conduct reflect only the highest form of behavior. It would be more effective to use statements such as "Thank you for putting the scissors in the box, Don. You might make a count of them, so we know how many we have," rather than "O.K., I know you kids are stealing the scissors! If I catch you, it won't be very funny."

4 Give the offending student an opportunity to return the stolen article to a certain unpoliced place, between certain hours, and with no questions asked. The article could even be mailed to a designated place. Generally, it is more important to reclaim the article than to identify the thief.

5 Reduce stealing through preventive efforts, such as emphasizing self-concept-building techniques and a sense of group responsibility and mutual respect.

6 Report the incident to the police and cooperate with them.

7 Role play (see Appendix) incidents that demonstrate that in our culture stealing has strong consequences. For example, take a current story from the news media to dramatize. Most newspapers provide ample material!

8 Try bibliotherapy (see Appendix) using stories about Honest Abe or other, less pointed, material.

9 Use class discussions (see Appendix) to explore reasons people steal. Identify constructive ways to meet people's needs. The discussions could conceivably lead to a unique plan to decrease thievery in your class or school.

STEPCHILDREN

SEE ALSO
Changing Family Structure
Stress

CAPSULE: A stepchild is a member of a family in which at least one of the adults is a stepparent and one or both of the adults has a child by a former marriage or relationship. The combined family is fast becoming the dominant form of the family. Today, more than 50 percent of marriages end in divorce. Of those, 80 percent of divorced persons will remarry within three years and nearly half of the second marriages will end in divorce after four years. One out of every six American children under eighteen is a stepchild. The prime reasons given for family breakups are money and the children. Children, caught in the middle, often feel responsible for the breakup.

The dynamics of stepfamilies are complex. When two separate family units merge, the stress factor heightens. Sheer numbers complicate the day-to-day operations of living, for there are the former spouses, grandparents, stepgrandparents, aunts, uncles, cousins, and others who have a lineal connection to the child and view their input as important. Sometimes, because of the extra stressors, the family with stepmembers becomes dysfunctional, unable to allow individuals to assert themselves, be listened to, and resolve problems.

Not all stepfamilies face insurmountable problems. Many make valiant efforts to make a new marriage work and are successful. Those are the ones that value the worth of each person, seek professional help when needed, and avail themselves of support groups and services when needed.

O P T I O N S

1 Allow your students to talk about their stepfamilies and help them to know that they are not alone in feeling confused about life.

2 Be aware that ambivalence is common in children who are pushed to merge into new family units just when they may be entering adolescence and are naturally bent on separation.

3 Encourage children of stepfamilies to start a support group, supervised by a counselor or teacher.

4 Remember that stepchildren have more than two parents to consider when making presents, invitations, or cards.

5 Take steps to see that school forms are printed to accommodate several names in the spaces for information.

6 Use bibliotherapy (see Appendix).

STRESS

SEE ALSO
Anxiety
Drug Use
Jealousy

CAPSULE: One all-encompassing and wry definition of stress is the following: a nonspecific response to a certain demand at any one time! According to some authorities on stress, the only way to avoid it is to be dead. It is part of the human condition from beginning to end. No one escapes it, nor should they want to: for stress is both necessary and dangerous.

Stress is healthy when a good match exists between the stressors and the person's ability to cope. The increasingly complex demands of a fast-paced society affect children and their parents equally. If anything, the younger generation has a more difficult time because they may feel that they have less control of their world.

Typical stressors for children include divorce, a family move, change in family income, a new baby, death of a sibling, death of a pet, change of school, academic difficulties, racial strife, and peer pressure. Symptoms of stress in students include sleeplessness, extreme fatigue, escape behavior (excessive daydreaming, watching too much TV), clinging to another person, and acting-out behavior.

O P T I O N S

1 Be aware that excessive stress is an invitation to drug use.

2 Encourage students to manage stress through both physical and mental coping techniques. Emphasize a balanced diet, exercise and rest, time management, goal setting, and breathing and muscle control.

3 Note students' complaints. Headaches, stiff necks, shoulder pains, stomachaches, scowling, and rubbing head and shoulders are all symptoms of stress.

4 Recognize sudden crying or other emotional outbursts as possible indicators of stress.

5 Reduce causes of stress (stressors) whenever possible. For example, high-school students who feel overwhelmed academically may be able to drop elective courses to lessen pressure.

6 Reinforce students' successes. Successful coping diminishes the extent of stress.

7 Remember "managing stress" does not mean *eliminating* it, but *handling* it.

8 Study students' conduct with an eye to discerning whether irresponsible behavior or pent-up anger may connote stress. Tap the resources of the counseling department.

STUBBORNNESS

SEE ALSO
Argumentativeness
Compulsiveness
Fearfulness
Maturational Delay

CAPSULE: Stubbornness is sometimes called the debatable virtue. Take, for example, the mother who confers with the teacher. During their discussion, the mother refers to the child's stubbornness as being tinted with independence, resolution, and stalwartness, and she may even coyly volunteer that she "was a bit like that" herself. Later on, the father of the child confers with the teacher and refers to the mulish stubbornness of the child, tainted by "the other side of the family." Tinted or tainted, the behavior exists.

One thing is certain, constant power struggles are counterproductive. They only worsen the situation as students show their need to be in control. Stubborn people are often highly intelligent and extremely competent in certain areas. When they are uncompromising within their particular realm of excellence, they receive support for behaving on a "matter of principle." When they habitually control others through stubbornness, they are not only difficult but also unfair to others. Consider the stubborn student a challenge. Chances are that under the cloak of obstinacy resides someone who wants sincere friendship, which you ought not stubbornly withhold.

OPTIONS

1 Acknowledge obvious efforts to be less stubborn. ("Cathy, you're to be commended for changing your mind and coming to the meeting. Your suggestion at the end really saved the day.")

2 Ask students to put into writing reasons they feel that they must stubbornly resist _____. Create a journal-writing assignment on a concrete issue or on the topic of stubbornness.

3 Avoid calling undue attention to stubborn students. Their stubborn conduct may soon pass. If too much is made of negative behavior, however, stubbornness may become a badge of distinctiveness.

4 Be willing to wait for students who stubbornly refuse to act. Waiting and silent periods are not devoid of thought. When the stubborn student does make a statement, empathize and reflect. ("I think I know what you mean when you say you won't play the game their way because _____.")

5 Deny the student certain privileges but offer alternatives, then be aware of opportunities to reinforce cooperative behavior.

6 Help the student see the difference between being stubborn and "standing up for one's rights." ("Pat, as soon as you mention 'rights' you are implying that others have them, too, and that means that you're traveling a two-way street. Let's focus on the *issue* and consider it a problem to be solved rather than a battle to be won.") Try a win/win strategy in which cooperation is emphasized and competition (the notion that one either wins or loses) is discarded.

7 Present a hypothetical case of extreme stubbornness and discuss it with the class.

8 Role play (see Appendix) an incident of obtuse stubbornness, such as a student refusing to move from a seat. Follow this activity with a class discussion.

9 Show films dealing with stubbornness and follow them with discussion.

10 Transfer the stubborn student to another class. Sometimes such a move brings about an unexplainable change in attitude and conduct.

STUDY SKILLS

SEE ALSO
Reading Problems

CAPSULE: Some students seem to speed through school effortlessly, while others encounter roadblocks throughout their education because they never master how to study. In our rapidly changing world, students need to learn how to learn in order to keep pace with their environment. Teachers and parents can provide concrete assistance so that students can "study smarter, not harder."

Good study skills help students to make efficient and effective use of their study time. Students should study with a plan and purpose and should be aware of specific strategies that work for them. Teachers can help by making course content interesting and relevant and by teaching and modeling study skills.

Librarians, both school and public, can also assist students to study smarter by showing them how to get the most out of educational resources. With the advent of learning, resource, and instructional materials centers, teachers and students should be well informed about new facilities and technologies that can enhance learning. Library and resource center staff members should be more committed to sharing information and learning strategies than to maintaining silence and order. The following suggestions may help to make studying more efficient.

O P T I O N S

1 Ask students to record on 3-by-5-inch notecards information to be memorized. Recall information includes formulas, vocabulary, names, quotations, etc. Students can use the easily portable notecards for quick refreshers while waiting for a bus, riding to and from school, etc.

2 Develop listening skills (see Appendix) through regular, brief exercises. Insist that students take notes during lectures and discussion. Explain which points are particularly important to guide students in what they should write down.

3 Discuss study skills in class. Allow students to share (in large or small groups) ways they have devised to learn various types of lessons.

4 Emphasize reading skills in which students analyze text structure. Help students find where main ideas are located in paragraphs. Give students assignments and practice in paraphrasing or summarizing what they have read or heard. Repeated practice will help students identify main points and important concepts.

5 Give students a learning-style inventory so that they can assess in which manner they learn best. The teacher can devise an inventory or can use those already on the market. (See Learning Styles, Appendix).

6 Help students allocate time and space for studying. Teach students how to use an assignment notebook and how to organize materials. Show students how to break large tasks into small, manageable components.

7 Instruct students to study with pencils or pens in their hands. Encourage them to create their own study guides through visual representations of course material. These outlines/pictures can take the form of graphic organizers or maps.

8 Involve parents in improving study skills. Hold a general parent meeting to share the study strategies the children are receiving. Many parents are perennial students themselves and may find study suggestions helpful.

9 Show students a process for seeking help. Encourage them to ask for teacher or other school staff assistance and to form peer study groups.

10 Suggest to students that they prepare for a test according to the format of the test. For example, for an upcoming essay test, students might predict sample questions and write sample answers. For short-answer tests, students can take brief notes of important points. For oral tests, students can practice relaying concepts and explanations out loud.

11 Teach a specific skill in connection with a given assignment. ("Today we will learn legal-type note-taking in connection with our social studies assignment.") (See Legal-type Note-taking, Appendix.) Remember that one-shot lessons are useless; the skill must be honed through regular practice.

STUTTERING

SEE ALSO
Speech Problems

CAPSULE: Stuttering is a stress signal. Some think that students who stutter never speak normally, even when talking to themselves. But this is not true; just as it takes two to tango, it takes two to stutter, a speaker and a listener. Many also believe that physical weakness may cause stuttering, but that position is not scientifically supported. A stuttering problem usually begins when the child is about three years of age. Parents may become overly anxious about the lack of smoothness in their child's speech and convey this concern to the child, who in turn becomes concerned about not speaking correctly, and the cycle continues. The parents and teachers working with the child who stutters need to learn to appreciate how children develop normal speech patterns and to be encouraged to leave the child's speech alone. Under no circumstances should children who stutter be ridiculed or forced into humiliating situations. Nor should their ideas be anticipated and stated for them. Students who stutter should be referred to qualified speech therapists for diagnosis and treatment. Following are some suggestions that may help children who stutter enjoy school more as well as improve their speech patterns.

OPTIONS

1 Assure students that they are making gains. ("You're speaking more smoothly all the time. Remember, it's okay to be hesitant in your speech. Everybody else hesitates, so why shouldn't you?")

2 Enlist with sincerity and discretion the cooperation of the other students in not ridiculing those who stutter and in listening when they speak. Train all students to give positive feedback to all student speakers, including those who stutter.

3 Provide many opportunities to increase confidence and decrease self-consciousness through group work, such as choral reading or glee club. The student who stutters can read along with tapes of good speaking models, such as Basil Rathbone's recordings of classical poetry and prose.

4 See that the children who stutter have many opportunities, separated by brief time intervals, to talk to people they *really like* in situations where they are *comfortable*.

SUICIDE

CAPSULE: Suicide among teenagers is second only to accidents as a cause of death. Multiple causes for teenage suicide include family disruption, academic pressures, loss of friends or feelings of having no friends at all, substance abuse, and fear of the future.

The shock of suicide often takes families and friends by surprise, but usually, in retrospect, several signs might have alerted them, such as (1) depression, (2) sharp changes in behavior (eating, sleeping habits), (3) academic failure, (4) break-up of friendships, (5) family problems (divorce, alcoholism, sexual abuse), (6) written notes or messages indicating a feeling of worthlessness, or (7) giving away personal belongings.

On record are numerous attempts at suicide by children in the preteen age group. In some cases the effort results in death, though more often the action is a desperate cry for help. Today, some schools have initiated suicide prevention programs. Some measures should be taken *cautiously* when suicide is only a suspicion; other measures should be taken *promptly* when suicide seems imminent.

O P T I O N S

1 Alert the school doctor, nurse, or counselor to your concerns regarding a potentially suicidal student.

2 Be aware that the student body contains vulnerable students. Engage students in sharing concerns so that they may come to realize that everyone has similar concerns and mood swings, *varying only in degree.*

3 Communicate frequently with parents to share concerns. Encourage parents to be open and attentive to their children's problems.

4 Consider contacting the student's church, synogogue, or civic organization leader. Use the utmost discretion.

5 Encourage your district to offer stress management workshops for students, faculty, and administrators.

6 Hold a staff meeting to discuss the student. (See Appendix). When several concerned adults share perceptions, they can work out a series of consistent strategies to help the student.

7 Investigate the availability of support groups for suicidal students. They will doubtless have some expertise in dealing with prevention programs to reduce "imitation suicides."

8 Listen carefully and actively to troubled students. Be careful about promises to "tell no one." Sometimes a warning to parents, counselors, or authorities may help save a young person's life.

9 Make an effort to spend some informal time with students who show signs of depression. Note the tenor of their conversations.

10 Refer to the school's plan for dealing with suicides where prevention and intervention efforts were not successful. Important: If no such crisis intervention plan is in place, the administration and faculty should devise one NOW.

11 Remember that teens talk to their friends before teachers or parents, so the friend may be a swift avenue to reaching the potential suicide.

12 Watch for signs of potential suicide in student writing. In a cry for help, students will sometimes provide signals in written compositions, such as narratives or journals.

Susceptible Children

SEE ALSO
Drug Use

CAPSULE: Susceptible children are sensitive and capable of submitting to enticing stimuli without thinking about consequences. They are easily duped by advertising in magazines, telephone solicitation, and television. Those good at conning such people detect them easily and take advantage of them before they know they've been taken. Susceptible individuals need help in differentiating between truth and blatant propaganda. They also need help in curbing their appetite for whatever has instant appeal and in delaying gratification.

OPTIONS

1 Dispense, deliberately, sound information and advice regarding judgment and wisdom in dealing with the social and business world.

2 Present to the class persuasive appeals used in the media. Ask students to analyze how emotions and behavior are manipulated through such appeals.

3 Use cooperative learning and class discussions (see Appendix) to resolve hypothetical situations pertaining to the pressures of advertising and peer pressure to acquire material goods.

TALKING *INCESSANT*

SEE ALSO
Blurting Out
Talking Out

CAPSULE: Nonstop talkers constantly verbalize because they crave attention and they do not know how to get it any other way. As long as they are filling the air with verbosity, they feel as if they are important. This behavior can be extremely distracting and detracts from the learning process. The constant pattern of nonstop talking can be more disruptive than the occasional interruption of "blurted out" responses or comments.

OPTIONS

1 Discuss excessive talking behavior one-on-one with the student. Set a limit for how many times that student can talk during a lesson. Remind students when they are past their allotted number of "contributions." Refuse to recognize them and insist that they remain silent. If students show improvement in self-discipline, compliment them privately and recognize their accomplishments.

2 Give talkers positive reinforcement for tasks they do well. Be free with compliments. ("José, I am truly impressed by the way you solved the math problems. The neatness also made your papers a pleasure to grade.") Because excessive talkers crave attention, if they receive recognition for accomplishments, their verbalizing may diminish.

3 Isolate the nonstop talker from friends in the classroom. Change the seating arrangement, if necessary.

4 Use cooperative learning groups in class (see Appendix). When students are assigned specific roles, such as recorder or time-keeper, they need to concentrate on defined tasks, which makes excessive talking difficult or impossible.

TALKING OUT

SEE ALSO
Blurting Out
Talking, Incessant

CAPSULE: Talking out differs from blurting out only in degree—the blurting is more like an explosion. Assume that the problem is solvable. Consider the possibility of a hearing problem. (Sometimes students with hearing impairments speak compulsively to fill the void.) Consider the balance and pace of the class structure: Are there ample periods of quiet? Of movement? Of group activity? Of discussion? We all need variety and spice in our lives. Perhaps the talker has decided to provide the spice because you have somehow overlooked it. Consider what students are telling you by talking out. ("I'm overstimulated by my neighbor." "I want to be liked." "I want attention." "I want to control you.") Be decisive. Students will readily understand that interferences with class routine must be dealt with because you have learning goals to achieve.

OPTIONS

1 Anticipate when a student is going to talk out. Say, "Jim, you had something to contribute."

2 Ask another teacher to observe your class. A colleague may notice something that has escaped your attention in dealing with the talker.

3 Ask the right questions. Well-phrased thought questions instead of fact questions may help to eliminate talking out. (See Inquiry Process and Bloom's Taxonomy, Appendix.)

4 Avoid statements like "Ben, you're always talking out." (He already knows that.) Instead, try "Ben, I've noticed several John Steinbeck books in your hands lately. Is this a new interest?"

5 Examine the class seating arrangement. Is the offending student perhaps sitting by a subtle contributor to the problem?

6 Ignore occasionally the student's attempts to get attention. Ask yourself, "Does this really interfere with the class's performance?"

7 Interpret for talkers what they have done. ("Andy, do you realize that by talking out just now you deprived Monica of a chance to tell us what she thinks?")

8 Provide the student with opportunities for talking within an acceptable framework.

9 Set aside ten minutes each day for *absolutely no talking*. Perhaps the class might engage in journal writing or sustained silent reading.

10 Try an approach that does not flatly deny the privilege of talking but that limits it. ("Alison, we only accept positive, constructive comments in this class.")

11 Try role playing (see Appendix). Offenders may gain some behavioral insights when their roles are taken by others.

12 Use class or small-group discussions (see Appendix) to uncover why there is so much talking out.

13 Work on a plan specifically designed for offending students. Talk to them privately and ask if they are aware of speaking out indiscriminately. Listen to them. Try to work out a reasonable plan to help them control talking out. ("I'm aware that we don't break old habits instantly, but we can try to make some changes a little at a time. Suppose I agree to ignore the first two times you talk out, but on the third time write your name on the board. Would that help?") Better still, encourage students to suggest their own plans of control.

TARDINESS

SEE ALSO
Absenteeism
Procrastination

CAPSULE: Chronic latecomers are saying something through their behavior, and the message can easily be misread. They might be seeking attention; they might be frightened of the day ahead because of failure to complete assignments; they might have been temporarily wooed away from school by a persuasive friend; they might have a substance abuse problem; or they might be delaying exposure to aversive behavior on your part. Students are tardy for a reason, so scrutinize the clues and work to change the behavior.

OPTIONS

1 Assure students that you recognize tardiness is a symptom of something but that you're not sure what it is. Maybe they can tell you!

2 Establish logical consequences for tardiness. ("Although I'm sure that no one in this class will ever want to be tardy, because our time together is important, any missed minutes at the beginning of the day will be made up in detention at the end of the day.")

3 Make sure that the first few minutes of class are significant. Start each lesson promptly with interesting, attention-getting activities so that students know that being late means missing out.

4 Show your pleasure when a usually tardy student is punctual, but don't overdo it, and never be sarcastic. One foolish remark like "So you decided to join us on time since we're having a party," means that you have lowered yourself to negative behavior.

5 Study the student's past performance and attendance records for clues. Don't fall into the trap of those who don't want to clutter their minds with any negative information from the student's past! Hold a staff meeting (see Appendix) to determine what kind of pattern exists.

6 Use students where you need assistance in extra capacities that will draw them to school on time: assistant cameraperson, audiovisual assistant, timekeeper for athletic events, and so on.

TATTLING

SEE ALSO
Loneliness
Rejected Children

CAPSULE: Tattling is common among the very young because it is an almost sure-fire attention getter. The tattletale is hard to ignore and loves to curry favor by peddling juicy morsels. Some will desist when peer pressure gets to them, but the persistent tattler says, in effect, that the scorn from peers is a small price to pay for the attention and reinforcement from adults. Sometimes the tattletale in school is looking for response from a parent figure; students will even tattle to incur punishment, which they may feel is deserved. Often the tattler feels unnoticed and unappreciated. Check your response to the talebearer; unwittingly we may convey the notion that we not only expect but actually enjoy the tales!

OPTIONS

1 Become aware of the student's social status with peers and when possible, redirect hostility. If, for instance, a tattler is on the same team with a persistent antagonist, consider a change.

2 Keep a mental record of tattlers' tales and, when appropriate, praise them for refraining from tattling.

3 Marshal the cooperation of colleagues and parents so there is unified resistance to tattling. What doesn't succeed won't continue.

4 Refuse to listen to one student's negative comments about another. By not reinforcing tattling, you can establish a climate where positive communication is valued and mutual respect is the norm.

5 Remind students that tattling is unacceptable behavior in school and that it is different

from reporting. ("Jackie, see if you can tell me which of these statements is tattling and which is reporting: 'James pulled Jan's hair' and 'Mrs. Brand said to tell you the bus is here.'"

6 Role play (see Appendix) a tattletale incident.

7 Show tattlers you appreciate them at a time when they

are not bearing tales. Refrain from mentioning tattling!

8 Use class or small-group discussions to talk about the negative social consequences of being a messenger. Encourage students to enjoy recognition for their own accomplishments, not for bearing tales of others' negative actions.

TEASING

SEE ALSO
Attention Seeking
Physical Differences
Prejudice

CAPSULE: Teasing is a common form of attention seeking. An innocuous annoyance in its milder forms, when persistent and overdone, teasing can become harassment. Some children are taunted to such an extent that they resist going to school because of the teasing they will encounter. Students who have physical differences, such as obesity or a deformity, are particularly vulnerable. Boys teasing girls (and vice versa) about romances may be secretly relished. However, excessive teasing, of any sort, can lead to hurt feelings and animosity.

O P T I O N S

1 Agree with students on something they can do when they get teased. ("We've decided today that we'll 'stare down' teasers.")

2 Confer with teasing recipients to determine whether they are consciously or subconsciously doing something to elicit the teasing. Are students purposely drawing attention to themselves in inappropriate ways?

3 Encourage students to develop a "thick skin" and not be overly sensitive to good-natured teasing. Help students identify differences between friendly teasing and that which is derogatory or cruel.

4 Give teased students sample "scripts" to use with teasers. Sometimes the direct approach works. ("Your saying _____ about me hurts my feelings. Please don't say that again.")

5 Isolate the teaser and the teased after an incident and allow them to "talk things over." This technique can be effective with younger children who are quick to forget superficial troubles. Being alone in a closed room without supervision, and with no questions asked afterward, can make students feel responsible for their own behavior.

6 Role play (see Appendix) a teasing incident.

7 Speak plainly about the courtesy and respect expected from students. Elicit from class members ways in which they should behave when someone decides to tease them or classmates.

8 Talk to the teasers one-to-one or in small groups about the effect their behavior has on others. Sometimes insensitivity must be brought out into the open to be dealt with effectively.

TEENAGE PREGNANCIES

SEE ALSO
Sexual Assault

CAPSULE: Despite widespread dissemination of information through the media on birth control measures, the number of pregnancies occurring to unwed teenagers continues to rise. Clearly, certain young people choose to ignore the warnings and data available to them for many reasons. Some dismiss the facts in favor of instant gratification. Still others hold to the hope that they will be "lucky" and avoid the consequences of their actions. Others may feel that having a child will bring love into a loveless life. The social implications of children having children are becoming increasingly serious in terms of lawsuits, interrupted and inadequate schooling, subsequent low-paying jobs, or the dependency on welfare programs.

Schools cannot avoid direct confrontation with teen pregnancies. Once over the hurdle of accepting the pregnancies as a fact of life, schools have emphasized dealing realistically with the issue. Special programs enabling the pregnant student to continue her education have come into existence. Child-care facilities have emerged on or close to some schools, and local social services have collaborated with many schools in working with the young girl and her parents. More openness has become the trend.

But what about the teenage father? Sometimes he is difficult to identify or track down. Efforts to trace him, through legal notices in newspapers and blood tests, are often unproductive. The unwed father may be as uninformed about how to raise a child as the mother.

Studies indicate that the teenage male suffers emotional distress, knowing that the girl may be contemplating an abortion, may be disowned by her parents, may be physically abused by parents, or may even die in childbirth. Occasionally, the teen father is able and willing to contribute financial aid to the mother and child. In some instances, the newborn receives the father's name, which tends to create a bond between parent and child if contact is sustained.

Because of their youth and subsequent lack of maturity, teenagers may have little knowledge of child development and little direct experience with children unless they come from a large family. They are, moreover, going through an impatient phase of their own lives and so are not inclined to be very patient with a baby. Child abuse often results. Children raising children is a risky business.

O P T I O N S

1 Address issues of human sexuality in psychology, sociology, health, or child development classes. Discuss the emotional responses of males *and* females to pregnancy. Shared responsibility can change the picture. Give students examples of life-scenarios of pregnant couples and teenage parents. Inform students of all consequences of teenage pregnancy.

2 Provide birth control information through the school, in health or physical education classes.

3 Recognize that teens are often not as sophisticated as they appear and respond to their search for accurate information on personal problems. Avoid moralizing or imposing your values on them but encourage them to walk on high ground.

4 Refer the pregnant student (and father, if available) to a counselor, in school or private practice. She will need prenatal care as well as accurate information regarding her options.

TELEVISION
WATCHING *EXCESSIVE*

SEE ALSO
Self-Concept
Study Skills

C A P S U L E : Excessive television viewing has been blamed for society's tolerance of and conditioned responses to violence, illicit sex, and depravity. Especially with the advent of cable, young people can be exposed to behaviors on television that they might not otherwise see. Some parents use television as a babysitter. Children sit mesmerized by the television. Some students even call themselves "couch potatoes."

To some extent, the fascination with television has been diluted by the advent of the computer and popular home video games. Still, the average student watches TV twenty-three hours a week. Research is now relating the number of hours that children watch television to cholesterol risk. The inactivity of watching television, plus the temptation to eat rich, cholesterol-laden foods while viewing, can eventually elevate viewers' cholesterol levels.

Television does provide excellent opportunities for educational enrichment and pleasure. It also provides opportunities for thinking people to practice their decision-making skills. Healthy, functional families monitor the programming and the time spent in front of the television.

OPTIONS

1 Analyze in class selected programs and commercials so that students can understand better some of the messages they receive via television.

2 Engage in a little research study with your class. For example, half of the class could give up TV for a week; the other half of the class could watch a designated number of hours. Evaluate the attitudes, grades, or any x factor of both groups.

3 Help parents set up a system in which homework and quiet reading and/or study time precedes any time allocated for watching television. Encourage parents to model limited viewing. During the school week, television watching could be restricted to special programs or events.

4 Incorporate excellent television programs occasionally in lesson plans. Some programs will encourage active listening and critical thinking.

TEMPER TANTRUMS

SEE ALSO

Anger

CAPSULE: The student who has a temper tantrum is sounding an alarm in more ways than one. Everything else stops with the screaming, and the audience is fascinated with how the drama will end. The adult in charge has to be concerned with immediate and long-range goals. Tantrums usually occur among the very young (four- and five-year-olds), but they occasionally occur among older children as well. At any age, if they continue it is because they work. Of course, acquiescing to a child who screams and flails limbs about sometimes seems to be the most pragmatic course, particularly if there is an audience. However, cures for tantrums include ignoring them or isolating the tantrum thrower. In the classroom, be prepared to have your corrective strategy complicated by oversolicitous classmates who will want to respond to the tantrum thrower in one way or another. If this is the case, a quiet comment or two will normally elicit cooperation. Remember that tantrum behavior was learned and that it must now be unlearned via consistent, constructive treatment.

OPTIONS

1 Appeal to the tantrum thrower's ego with a matter-of-fact statement. ("Barbara, nobody enjoys the Barbara who throws tantrums, but everybody enjoys the helpful Barbara.")

2 Apprise the child of what to expect from tantrums. ("Julio, tantrums are annoying to everyone. Don't expect to get favors with them.")

3 Communicate to parents information regarding the child's behavior. Work with parents on establishing consistent rewards and

consequences related to behavior.

4 Discuss with the student harmless ways of expressing anger. ("The next time you feel you must lash out, you may use the punching bag in the gym.")

5 Explain to the child involved, when he or she is calm, what the consequences will be after the next tantrum. ("Jerry, perhaps this situation will never happen again, but I want you to know what will happen if it does: I will leave you alone until you stop screaming.")

6 Provide a "time out" period for the child who has lost behavioral control. Allow the child to leave the classroom (sent to a supervised area) and to return when composure is regained.

7 Use nonverbal modes of coping, such as signaling the other students to follow you quietly out of the classroom and closing the door behind you.

TERMINALLY ILL CHILDREN

SEE ALSO
Dealing with Death

CAPSULE: Occasionally, a terminally ill child will be enrolled in regular classes. Especially regarding victims of the AIDS virus, some parents of well children may react irrationally to including the special child in the school. Until only recently, many persons having any form of cancer were politely avoided or shunned. The terminally ill student deserves careful and compassionate consideration by faculty and students. When honesty prevails, the results can be beneficial to all concerned.

OPTIONS

1 Be alert to the possibilities of abandonment of the terminally ill student by others in the class. One to one or in small groups, try to sensitize members of the class to the ill child's situation.

2 Become acquainted with the stages of the grieving process: denial, anger, bargaining, depression, acceptance. Fine-tune your understanding of the student's stages of awareness.

3 Consider working with ill children through their creativity, written or artistic. Remember that spontaneous drawings reflect the child's psychological world. Persons trained in "reading drawings" can derive information for helping the whole child.

4 Hold a staff meeting (see Appendix) of the key people who will be dealing with the student.

5 Make sure everyone, from the top administrators on down, is fully aware of the case history of the student.

6 Remember that the student is no doubt aware of the imminence of death but isn't

likely to talk about it. Handle references to death discreetly without becoming maudlin.

7 Talk with the student about the content of work. ("I see you have a big dog in your picture. I wonder what he's going to do.")

8 Use the child's work (pictures, poems, essays) as a basis for communication with the parents.

TEST ANXIETY

SEE ALSO
Fearfulness
Stress

CAPSULE: Fear of taking tests is common among normal students. When it becomes highly acute, however, it can be labeled a phobia. No amount of ridicule or minimizing will eradicate the problem. It must be dealt with straightforwardly, sympathetically, and systematically if it is to be conquered. The wise teacher will, of course, try to become well acquainted with the student's school record, noting such items as absences, grades in the different subject areas, and various potentiality indicators.

OPTIONS

1 Administer nontraditional (oral, pictorial) tests to the student to get a more complete measurement of intelligence and knowledge.

2 Administer untimed tests in order to eliminate timing frustration.

3 Allow students to feel that they have some control over the situation and solicit suggestions from them for conquering the problem.

4 Consider the use of appropriate background music during testing. Soft classical music may relax students and stimulate their right-brain hemispheres.

5 Contact a phobic student's parents for further information and cooperation.

6 Give students many opportunities to practice various test forms. Once students know how to attack tests according to format, they will feel more secure and comfortable.

7 Help the student work through an objective test, just for practice.

8 Remember to reinforce good performance on essay tests with written comments or verbal praise.

9 Talk to anxious students privately. Discuss fear of testing, reflecting their feelings. ("Taking tests really frightens the daylights out of you.")

As a result of your discussion, design a plan to attack the problem. It may involve steps in which the intensity gradually increases so that success is built into the program: (1) Take oral tests until able to handle the written. (2) Stay in the room, merely observing classmates taking a test. (3) Take bite-sized tests, then work up to more substantial ones.

10 Teach the student how to keep an assignment book.

11 Teach legal-type note-taking (see Appendix) to help the anxious student prepare better for tests.

Tics

SEE ALSO
Anxiety
Eye Problems

CAPSULE: Tics are small involuntary muscle spasms that sometimes evoke smiles, if not laughter, from the uninformed who think the person is trying to be funny by lifting eyebrows, blinking, head jerking, or even tongue clicking. Such behavior is not uncommon during adolescence, which one might expect, since pressures are high at this time of life. Actually, the tic operates both as an indicator of tension and as a safety valve. Be alert to the kinds of circumstances and types of personalities that seem to trigger the tic. If possible, exercise control of situations so that the behavior does not increase. Refrain from calling undue attention to a student's tic. Ordinarily, abstaining from any action is wise, but under certain circumstances it may be appropriate to try one of the following.

O P T I O N S

1 Arrange for a family consultation in order to learn the student's history.

2 Discuss with the class people's needs to release tension and hold a group sharing of different forms of adjustment. ("Today we are discussing some of our individual ways of coping with tension and nervousness. Jessica, you told me the other day that when you get nervous you move your left shoulder up and down and it's hard to stop it.")

3 Encourage kindness and tolerance among classmates. Asking students to "stop twitching" or "stop making noises" may cause students to tic even more.

4 Introduce a graduated and less-threatening approach to classwork. If, for instance, Sam is anxious about speaking before the class, have him privately record his speech on tape, then deliver it in a room by himself, then to a classmate, and finally to the entire class.

5 Refer the student to a physician for diagnosis. Multiple tics, involuntary body movements, or uncontrollable vocalizations and verbalizations may be characteristics of Tourette's syndrome, a neurological disorder. A physician may prescribe medication that suppresses symptoms, but does not cure the disorder.

6 Show students that you like and approve of them and that you can see past their differences.

Transient Children

CAPSULE: Today's families are movers. One statistic says Americans move, on the average, fifteen times in their lifetimes. Therefore, children rarely remain in one school system for their basic education, kindergarten through high school graduation.

Mobility, particularly in the urban areas, presents huge problems for school systems. Moves increase as incomes change. Children constantly on the move suffer a high degree of stress created by the need to find new friends, adjust to the academic rigors of a different school, and be accepted by new teachers. But not all children suffer from being uprooted; some thrive on it!

OPTIONS

1 Determine, as soon as possible, new students' academic skills. If necessary, design a program to help transient children to reach the academic level of their classmates.

2 Help set some goals for the new student. If some deficits are obvious (such as reading or math skills), arrange for special help.

3 Recognize students who have just moved into the community and make them feel welcome. Do the same with the parents.

4 Set up a buddy system or a peer mentor program (see Appendix).

5 View the new students as a resource, not a problem. Allow them to share something about the places they came from. Perhaps new students can be a multicultural resource in the classroom.

TRUANCY

SEE ALSO
Absenteeism
Fearfulness

CAPSULE: Students "cut" school for many reasons. Some of the causes of truancy are obvious (learning problems, fear of someone, irrelevancy of schoolwork, drug or gang-related problems), but others are more difficult to pinpoint. Preaching to the truant student is useless, as is retribution. The most practical course of action is to discover why the student chooses not to attend school and to work on the causes of truancy. Students want to feel welcome in school, and they need to see school's relevance in their own lives.

Depending on your philosophy, your type of school, and your understanding of the total problem, you may wish to try your version of some of the following suggestions.

OPTIONS

1 Be positive. Avoid sarcastic, aversive behavior. Comments such as, "So, you decided to come to school today!" only confirm that you don't like students, so why should they bother?

2 Counsel truants in a group setting, stressing values. Elicit from students ways of decreasing truancy. Respect and try their suggestions, even if they sound crazy to you.

3 Demonstrate to students that you are glad they're in school *without saying so*. Possible methods include asking them to take messages to important people, displaying their work without fanfare, using their names frequently, and being courteous when you address them.

4 Detain the truant in school after hours. *Caution:* The risks are great, since after-

school jobs, clearance with parents, sports, and club activities are common reasons (or excuses) for not staying. Too often, detention halls become places to put in time or just to sit. In a quiet setting supervised by a nonhostile person, a detention hall *can* be a good place for a truant to study and to take the consequences of voluntary misbehavior.

5 Discuss truancy freely in class (see Class Discussion, Appendix). Be alert to expressions of fears that cause students to avoid school.

6 Engage peer mentors (see Appendix) to work with truants as individuals or in a group. High-school peer mentors working with students younger than themselves can be very effective. Encourage them to devise their own motivating techniques.

7 Establish a new kind of relationship with the truant. Spend time talking with the student, one-to-one, outside of class.

8 Evaluate with truant students their academic work. Explain the academic impor-tance of being in class and that grades might have been higher with better attendance.

9 Examine the pattern of a truant's absences and use it as a topic for discussion. If, for example, the absences are always on exam days, try "Jenny, I've observed that your last three absences were on days Mr. Hill had a chemistry test scheduled. Does that mean anything, or is it just a coincidence?"

10 Explain the school rules that are absolutely firm. At the same time, tell students the areas in which they can establish rules and how to go about doing so (such as through the student council, petitions, or lobbies).

11 Hold a staff meeting (see Appendix) with the truant student and parents present. The adult who has the best relationship with the student might chair the meeting. Open discussion should precede formulation of a reasonable plan of action.

12 Individualize the truant's instruction (see Flight Plan, Appendix). Personalizing the lessons is one way to keep the schoolwork relevant to the student's life.

13 Make available to the truant responsible jobs that will demand being in school (handling physical education, audiovisual, or stage equipment, for example).

14 Make truancy a subject of research and discussion in the class's course of study.

15 Refer to a ladder of offenses and their corresponding results. (First offense: student is warned by school personnel; second offense: parent is notified by telephone in the presence of the student [a letter is sent if there is no phone]; third offense: student, parents, and teacher[s] confer and agree upon a plan of action.) Such ladders can be constructed by a representative committee, can be circulated among students and parents, and can be referred to when a course of action needs to be taken.

16 Require the student to be responsible for work missed during absences. Some teachers complain about having to give extra time to a truant outside of class, while others welcome this opportunity to get some insight into the student's problems. Administrators can help their faculties by seeing that make-up work guidelines are carefully thought out and circulated.

17 Tell students directly that their presence is important and expected. Explain that teachers often view class cutting as a personal affront.

18 Threaten the student with consequences of further truancy. *Caution:* People who threaten usually overuse the technique. Occasionally, however, a threat, with follow-through, is quite effective.

19 Work on making lessons enjoyable and relevant and class climate warm and inviting so that students will not want to miss class.

TWINS

SEE ALSO
Sibling Rivalry

CAPSULE: Multiple births have been documented throughout history, but with the advent of successful fertility treatments the numbers have increased. Twins occur about once in ninety-six births; triplets, quadruplets, and quintuplets less frequently. The two general types of twins are *fraternal* and *identical.*

The unique closeness and like-mindedness of identical twins have given rise to extremely interesting studies of human behavior and the eternal "nature vs. nurture" debate. For instance, some reports reveal that twins separated at birth and adopted into geographically separated families not only married spouses who were very similar, but also gave their children similar or identical names, developed like tastes in color and decorating, and even pursued the same careers.

In early childhood, identical twins sometimes develop a language all their own, one that not even the mother can understand. Sometimes it takes a sibling a year or two older to interpret for the parents!

Special considerations should be taken into account when enrolling twins in school. Current educational philosophy supports placing the children in different classes, if possible, in order to nurture their individual personalities.

If twins are identical, their classmates enjoy looking for minute traits to differentiate them, as do their teachers. Even so, fun-loving siblings will find ways to confound their peers and teachers by switching seats, answering for one another, and keeping everyone guessing!

O P T I O N S

1 Accept twins as you do any other students. Avoid making comparisons.

2 Be sensitive to the special bond that identical twins share and expect them to defend one another fiercely. (That may not be at all true of fraternal twins, who may not even look alike or have similar personalities.)

3 Encourage the development of each twin's confidence and individuality. Reinforce individual strengths and preferences.

UNATTRACTIVE CHILDREN

SEE ALSO
Name Slurring
Physical Differences
Prejudice

CAPSULE: Research indicates that physically attractive children are viewed by society as more intelligent than others and are expected to live up to that expectation. It follows that people develop self-image and personality traits that reflect their degree of attractiveness. The unattractive child has responses going in the opposite direction. And they hurt!

Combating an unattractive child's misery requires that parents and teachers begin with their own feelings about the child and place value on the inner self rather than the outward appearance. An emphasis on words and deeds, not appearance, must be clearly conveyed to the students.

OPTIONS

1 Ask children who insult an unattractive classmate *why* they did it. Involve children in a discussion to elicit the feelings involved when one person attacks another. (See Class Discussions, Appendix.)

2 Reexamine your attitudes toward unattractive students. Make sure that positive non-verbal responses are not distributed according to students' physical attractiveness.

3 Remember that discrimination against physically unattractive children may have long-term effects. A brush-off, a slur, or a condescending remark has enormous staying power that lasts into adulthood.

4 Work with parents on ways to bolster students' self-esteem. In some cases, cosmetic changes through orthodontics or minor surgery can make a student look and feel more attractive.

UNDERACHIEVERS

SEE ALSO
Anxiety
Fearfulness
Reading Problems
Self-Concept

CAPSULE: Underachieving describes many of us. In school jargon the term is used to describe a discrepancy between the mental age (as reflected in an intelligence test [IQ] score) and the educational age (as reflected in standardized achievement test scores). For instance, a student with an IQ of 100 whose achievement test scores are in the thirtieth percentile is underachieving. Chances are, underachievement is related to socioeconomic factors, family factors, unrealistic goals, or a poor self-image. The reasons could also be physical, in which case referral to the school or family doctor is appropriate. In American culture, boys outnumber girls as underachievers until late in high school. Cultural taboos that might lead to underachievement, such as labeling fields of study more appropriate for one sex or another, still prevail—but they are gradually being lifted.

Research does not discount the fact that teachers' and parents' attitudes and expectations affect the performance of the student. Sometimes underachievers are fulfilling the expectations of those around them as in the case of the student who constantly hears that he or she couldn't possibly perform as well as a sibling who was in that room last year. After checking the difficulty level of the subject matter and the pace that you adhere to in your classroom, you might help underachievers by (1) focusing on activities that help them establish attainable goals, (2) reinforcing what is already admirable in their performances, and (3) undergirding their self-images with pride. Being a motivator instead of a manipulator is one of your first responsibilities. The following ideas can be cut to size for all ages.

OPTIONS

1 Assign journal-writing activities in which students express how they feel about their progress in school. Students may be able to articulate causes for underachievement.

2 Become aware of any exaggerated fears underachievers may have related to schoolwork, and lead them gradually through a process that conquers their fears.

3 Check the underachieving student's ability to read by giving, or asking the reading specialist to administer, a reading inventory that will indicate frustration, instructional, and independent reading levels.

4 Confer with the parents and urge them to converse with their underachieving children about school. Caution parents to avoid asking questions such as, "What did you learn in school today?" Children are sure to say, "Nothing." Instead, suggest something such as, "You played hard in that after-school game." This kind of statement opens lines of communications instead of turning them off.

5 Consider adjusting the curriculum to better serve the underachiever. Incorporate activities that appeal to varied learning styles (see Learning Styles, Appendix). Students may achieve better

when instruction corresponds to how they learn best.

6 Encourage the student who underachieves to commit to improvement (see Commitment Technique, Appendix): "I agree to check all of my math before handing in my assignments. I further agree to meet Mrs. Smith, my math teacher, for a conference every Thursday at 2:00 for the next three weeks." *Caution:* It is easy for a student to be extravagant when drawing up a contract, so encourage realistic goals and activities.

7 Have the student maintain an assignment book. The teacher initials this book each time the student has entered an assignment correctly; the parents initial it each time the student has finished an assignment.

8 Have the underachiever work with another student. Peers can often provide the impetus to spark achievement.

9 Hold a staff meeting (see Appendix) to discuss the best strategy to be used with the underachievers. Be sure the students are accountable to the people who work best with them.

10 Note an underachiever's outside-of-school interests and relate academic work to these. Construct a flight plan (see Appendix) based on the student's interest areas. This plan enables the student to see the total assignment and adjust the work schedule accordingly.

11 Refer the underachieving student to a counselor at school.

12 Reflect the student's feelings about achievement. Use active listening. ("You don't feel satisfied with your work in English, but you're at a loss as to how to improve.") If the student seems to find in you someone who understands, you may have your first opportunity to give specific assistance.

13 Reinforce the underachiever's lessons with honest, substantive praise. ("Ted, in only ten minutes you have finished three out of four problems. Get yourself a drink, and let's see what you can accomplish in the next ten minutes.")

14 Teach the student some specific skills. (See study skills, Appendix.)

15 Use an extrinsic reward (see Appendix) to motivate the underachiever. ("Every time

you improve in
_____, you will
receive a token. When you
accumulate twenty tokens
you may exchange them for
_____.")

16 Use a student self-rating
technique. Once a week, for
example, the student evalu-
ates progress made with an
adult. Encourage the student
to devise a self-rating tool, a
chart or graph that registers
changes in achievement.

17 Use brainstorming (see
Appendix) to collect the students' ideas regarding effective class-as-a-whole motivation. ("In the next seven
minutes each group will list
as many ideas as possible
that could be used to motivate learning in this class.")
Next, share, thrash out, and
agree upon some viable
steps for implementing the
best ideas. Follow this procedure with evaluation.

VANDALISM

SEE ALSO
Gangs

C A P S U L E : Vandalism is on the increase. Inside and out, many schools and other public and private buildings bear the scars of ruthless disregard for others' property. This fact poses some questions, among them: "Are the schools indeed breeding this hostile behavior?" and "Can the schools rectify the situation?" The respective answers are, "Sometimes" and "Possibly." At any rate, schools and parents must work together to solve the problem.

Unlike the arsonist, who prefers to work alone or with one accomplice, the vandal usually goes with a group. Vandals dwell in a world of ambivalence, for in their bid for attention they fear getting caught, yet hope they will be.

Flagrant abuse of property raises the ire of thinking, feeling people. Sympathy for the vandal runs thin when smashed windows, rifled offices, destroyed computers, besmirched walls, defaced books, and slashed tires are left in their wake. The immediate impulse, and doubtless the correct move, is to contact the police. However, the school cannot rest the case there; it must examine possible factors within the school that might be contributing to such aggressive conduct. In other words, the disease, not the symptom, must be treated. This calls for a united faculty-student effort that emphasizes restitution instead of retribution.

OPTIONS

1 Ask students to suggest what they feel is appropriate compensation for their misdemeanors. Keep the compensation appropriate to the offense, preferably in terms of work rather than of money. ("Tom, you defaced the flagpole and you feel it is fair to expect you to paint it," or "You scratched the table and now you will sand it.")

2 Ask students to write descriptions of their acts of vandalism. Place the descriptions in students' files and agree to remove them at the end of the school year if and when students have not repeated acts of vandalism.

3 Challenge the student by interpreting his or her strategy. ("You know, Dee, by scratching notes all over the outside of the building you must be giving a distress signal. Perhaps you can tell me what it is.")

4 Confer with the principal or other administrators. They may enlist the cooperation of law-enforcement officers.

5 Consult the guidance counselor.

6 Discuss values informally. ("Today we are going to consider the subject of property. First, list ten items of property that you take good care of. Next, list ten items that you are careless with. After each listing, put an M if the property is yours, an O if it belongs to others, and a P if it is public property.")

7 Emphasize career guidance. The student who has a constructive world-of-work goal will have little time for vandalism.

8 Engender a spirit of pride in the school by making different individuals, classes, or clubs responsible for some of the building and ground care. Primary-grade children can select a bush to plant and nurture, for example. They can put name tags on trees or near flowerbeds to personalize and generate pride in responsible acts that give pleasure to the entire school.

9 Fine the offending student so that repairs or replacement can be made.

10 Have the student body sponsor an annual "Spring Housecleaning Day." The student council could plan and execute the activity, and chairmanship could be on a yearly rotating basis (this

year the seniors, next year the juniors, and so on). A field-day event could climax the day.

11 Invite professionals (such as psychologists and psychiatrists) from the community to speak to your class about destructive, aggressive behavior.

12 Notify the parents of a vandalous student. Arrange a conference with the parents and the student. *Note:* Your particular school policy will determine who notifies the parents and who holds the conference.

13 Recognize, and give credit for, obvious efforts to resist temptations to deface property and obvious efforts to discourage others from vandalism. ("I saw you discourage Sandy from dragging her pencil along the hall wall. Thank you!")

14 Use a student court to deal with the vandal.

15 View and acknowledge scribbling and scratching activities for what they are. One cannot label the teenager who scratches his and his girlfriend's initials on his notebook a vandal. When the scratches become offensive words and are carved on public property, *that* is vandalism!

WANDERERS

SEE ALSO
Dawdling
Restlessness
Tardiness

CAPSULE: Wanderers don't run away; they only avoid what they should be doing. Every school has a few. They eventually become known, but at first they may be cheerful volunteers who will run errands for the teacher, or ask what they can do to help—the all-around teachers' pets. When word gets around that these students stopped by to look in on several other classes, browsed a while in the library, went to the restroom, had a chat with the custodian, checked out the lockers, had a long drink, and came back with a nonchalant air, everyone knows they are wanderers.

Wanderers enjoy being on the move, away from structure. They've figured out that starting out with a legitimate motive (delivering a message to the principal, for instance) gives them license to move through the halls without supervision. Meanwhile, they may be satisfying curiosity about how the school is run.

OPTIONS

1 Allow no one out of the classroom except in cases of emergency.

2 Deal directly with itinerant students regarding wandering around, bothering other classes, and wasting time. Let them know that others in the school are aware of their behavior and that they must discipline themselves to change. Be mindful that students, particularly the very young, may not have considered that they were doing anything out of line just because they like to poke around.

3 Retrain the identified wanderer. ("Jamie, we have only five minutes before we'll begin the film. Could you take this to Miss Dole for me and come right back?")

4 Use hall passes that must be signed (with the time) by an adult at the student's destination. This creates a record of when and where students move throughout the school.

5 Use a sign-out and sign-in sheet for going to the bathroom.

WASTEFULNESS

CAPSULE: With its abundant resources, our nation has spawned people who take much for granted. While the schools (particularly public schools) may have unwittingly contributed to the belief in a bottomless storehouse by providing ample tax-paid supplies, we now must teach conservation and frugality. Many teenagers are ecology minded, and on their own have instituted worthwhile projects. The younger students need prudent training and good examples to follow.

O P T I O N S

1 Begin a recycling campaign in school. Paper, aluminum cans, and certain plastic items can be kept in special containers and recycled through city or private companies.

2 Discuss shortages of all kinds (gas, water, toilet paper) and encourage the students to speculate on the consequences that might ensue if present trends continue unabated.

3 Discuss signs of excess in society (eating and drinking habits, for example).

4 Encourage students to think of as many ways as they can to use wastepaper, pencil shavings, stubby pencils, wrappers, and boxes. While engaged in such divergent thinking, they may become fascinated with the possibilities for other kinds of leftovers.

5 Lead the students into the habit of salvaging bits and pieces of things. Store things in a categorized manner (crayons, fabric, and string, each in separate boxes) so that students will have ready access to them.

6 Limit the students to a specific quota of supplies and devise a fair, efficient way of dispensing them.

7 Show, by products you make, how things others might throw away can become part of an attractive display or a functional item.

8 Urge the student who crumples a little-used piece of paper to build a supply of scratch paper for working math problems.

WHINING

CAPSULE: Whining is the sound and sign of an unhappy person. People outside the school setting don't often have the patience to deal with whiners; they simply avoid them. This leaves the teachers and parents with the burden of effecting behavioral changes, if any are to be made. The problem is doubly difficult if the child's model happens to be a teacher or a parent! Hopefully, casual disregard for the whining will eventually eliminate it, but if it doesn't, try some of these ideas.

OPTIONS

1 Discuss whining behavior in a class meeting (see Appendix). ("The other day, when Mrs. Z. substituted, she said several children whined. Can we talk about why they did that?")

2 Emphasize to students that they can more often attain goals by positive behavior, as opposed to whining and complaining.

3 Reinforce nonwhiny behavior with a compliment. ("Sara, did you realize that when you spoke to me just now, you didn't whine at all? Beautiful!")

4 Talk to the whiner about the habit and agree upon a silent, secret reminder to help break it. ("I'll put my pencil on my ear when I hear that unpleasant sound.")

5 Write the student's name, followed by a smiling face, on the board at the end of a nonwhiny day.

WITHDRAWN CHILDREN

SEE ALSO
Daydreaming

CAPSULE: To withdraw to a safe place when threatened by anything is normal defensive behavior. To
spend most of one's time in this manner is not normal.
In a secure nook of withdrawal, a person can dream
and fantasize, perhaps for long periods of time, without
detection. It can happen in the classroom, and it does.
Take note of the child who is described as "so good,"
"never gives anyone a minute's trouble," or "very shy
and sweet." That student could, in fact, be very well
adjusted but, on the other hand, excessively passive
behavior could be expressing such feelings as "I want
to be liked," "I'm afraid of being hurt," "I feel inferior to
others," "I can't do the work," "The work is dull," "The
courses have no relevance to my life," "I don't understand the teacher's speech pattern," or "I'm sick."

Explore the possibility that withdrawn behavior
has a physical basis. Sometimes students who act out
are much healthier than withdrawn ones, who may be
stockpiling emotions for eventual explosions.
Remember that since those students dwell in a fantasy
world, much of their activity will be covert. Such students usually function best in a classroom environment
that is uncluttered and structured.

If you are serious about helping the withdrawn
child, you will learn as much as you can from the usual
sources: records, parents, teachers, counselor, observation, and so on. You will carefully assess the difficulty

and amount of work for the student, remembering that work too easy or too difficult encourages withdrawal into less threatening realms. You will check into dietary habits, since research indicates that many tuned-out students overindulge in carbohydrates and sweets. You will find ways to show the student that you believe in the need to dream and fantasize but that you are convinced of the need for a healthy balance between dreaming and doing. You will be alert to young children's tendencies to overprotect a withdrawn classmate and to older students' inclinations to ignore their apathetic peer.

OPTIONS

1 Arrange to involve younger withdrawn students in puppetry, if not as puppeteers (where they have the security of a backstage station), then as viewers of a story about a character who is tuned-out, dreamy, passive, and so forth.

2 Ask the withdrawn student to tutor a younger student and help with the proper procedure. ("Eric, I've been asked by the second-grade teacher to find tutors for several children. May I submit your name to her?")

3 Capitalize on the children's chief interests, allowing them to pursue interests in seclusion; seize the right time to help them move into a small-group activity.

4 Design a flight plan (see Appendix) with the students. This activity approach enables them to emerge gradually.

5 Exercise skill in preparing withdrawn students for lesson transitions, since abrupt changes frighten them. ("Those who have finished reading the science directions may go for a drink and then join Jan's group to do the experiment.")

6 Find ways for the student to make a genuine contribution. ("Tom attended the horse races last month. I see a model of the winner on his desk. Can you tell us about his records, Tom?")

7 Get students started by physically placing them in position with paper, book, and pencil and posterior squarely on the chair (a dubious strategy with older students!).

8 Give the student a task that both teaches and requires physical movement (putting away cards in numerical order, for instance).

9 Give the student many opportunities to develop self- and critical judgment by selecting his or her own best work (best page, best picture, best letter, best anything). *Variation:* Help the student compare this month's record with last month's.

10 Give the student some responsibility, even if it has nothing to do with the lesson (collecting things, distributing things, counting things).

11 Have a fellow student work with the withdrawn child and praise the helper when the tuned-out one tunes in.

12 Hold out a simple reward. ("Tina, as soon as you finish this you may _____.")

13 Question the student after successful participation in a task, with "How does that make you feel?" This may prompt a feeling that withdrawing is not the only means of coping.

14 Show videotapes that depict children enjoying each other's company. Let the medium be the message.

15 Suggest something positive. ("Rick, tell me how far you've gotten in your math," instead of "Rick, stop daydreaming!")

16 Talk to the student privately about the tendency to daydream. Use active listening and restate the student's ideas nonjudgmentally. ("You like to dream about a world without schools.")

17 Use a reward system (see Extrinsic Rewards, Appendix) that encourages participation. ("Each time you work with another student you will receive _____," or "Each time you participate in class you will be credited with _____.") *Note:* Every plan must be tailor-made for the student and tempered with common sense.

18 Use a timer to keep the student's interest focused on a task. *Variations:* Establish time limits in odd minutes. ("Greg, how much can you finish in seven minutes?")

ANN LANDERS TECHNIQUE*

This technique sprang from necessity when a guest speaker failed to arrive in an auditorium packed with expectant students. Acting on an impromptu basis, a counselor took the microphone and asked, "Until our guest speaker arrives, would you like to fill in by posing a problem and getting some immediate response from the audience?" There was a resounding "Yes!" The counselor then established four ground rules:

1. The questioner must come to the platform and use the microphone.

2. The responders must come to the platform and use the microphone.

3. The responders must take their place in line at the side of the platform and await their turn.

4. The responders may speak one minute.

Someone dubbed the procedure the "Ann Landers technique," a name that stuck. This procedure can be helpful as part of an all-school guidance program.

Permission granted by Ann Landers and Creators Syndicate.

AUTHENTIC (ALTERNATIVE) ASSESSMENT

Authentic (Alternative) Assessment is the measuring of student learning in a variety of forms. Students can demonstrate learning through performances, artifacts, journals, or any number of art forms. The teacher clearly articulates criteria for assessment. Assessment criteria reflect an agreement between teacher and student about what is important in a student's work. Authentic assessment offers a broader perspective of evaluation than traditional paper and pencil tests do.

BIBLIOTHERAPY

Bibliotherapy is a technique designed to provide therapy through reading. A teacher or counselor selects specific literature to reinforce students' positive feelings about themselves. When students with serious personal problems read about someone who has demonstrated inordinate courage in facing a handicap, hazard, or emotional crisis, those students often gain courage to face their own problems.

Several excellent recommended lists of stories and books are available from commercial companies. They are complete with teacher's guides. The librarian in your school can be of enormous help in obtaining such a list for you or in compiling a recommended list from the existing library collection. The school counselor will also be able to assist you, since bibliotherapy is often used in working with parents.

BLOOM'S TAXONOMY

Bloom's taxonomy (named for its creator, educator and researcher Benjamin Bloom) is a ladder that reflects increases in the amount and nature of types of thinking. The taxonomy is a way to describe degrees of thinking according to a hierarchy. The hierarchy distinguishes between rote responses and responses that require a higher level of thought. The first two levels, knowledge and comprehension, require reproducing material from a source. The next two levels, analysis and application, require using material from a source to form a broader concept. The two highest levels, synthesis and evaluation, require integrating learned information in totally new concepts.

BRAIN PREFERENCE (HEMISPHERICITY)

Brain preference (hemisphericity) refers to learners' tendencies to use one side of the brain or the other in acquiring and integrating new information. Learners with right-brain tendencies prefer pictorial, schematic, big-picture exposure. Learners with left-brain tendencies prefer verbal, linear (sequential), small-component exposure. Teachers and parents can enhance learning through awareness of and appeals to the student's brain preference.

BRAINSTORMING

Brainstorming is a technique used to encourage people to share ideas without feeling foolish or self-conscious. Brainstorming rules include:

1. No censoring of ideas is allowed. Every idea is accepted.

2. Rapid-fire participation is encouraged. This relieves the temptation to sort out ideas, and it also keeps people on their toes.

3. Participants are encouraged to work on others' ideas. The group soon gets the feeling that while there may be "nothing new under the sun," new arrangements of old ideas spell creativity.

BUDDY SYSTEM

A buddy is an assigned friend equipped to help a new student adjust to a new environment with the least amount of stress. The school counselor can train buddies and assist teachers in pairing students. In addition to helping new students, buddies can help students with special needs or students for whom English is a second language. Buddies may also be assigned to inform fellow students about homework assignments during absences.

CLASS DISCUSSIONS

Class discussions can deal with the total range of the daily behaviors and concerns of students, teachers, and parents. The requirements of the discussions are simply stated but require patience and practice. They are: (1) the discussion content must be important and relevant; (2) the leadership must be nonjudgmental (no matter how difficult a task this is); and (3) all participants must be seated in a circle, which provides face-to-face relationships and is a movement in the direction of equal power.

COMMITMENT TECHNIQUE

The commitment technique of working with classroom behaviors is one of the approaches developed by William Glasser to implement his reality therapy. The major differences between this approach and other disciplinary approaches are that (1) it focuses on individual responsibility rather than punitive measures; (2) it directs attention to conscious behavior instead of unconscious thoughts and feelings; (3) it emphasizes the present, not the past; (4) it stresses children's needs for value judgment with regard to their own behavior; and (5) it actively teaches responsible behavior (via the plan and commitment) as opposed to allowing children to find their own way.

A simplification of the commitment technique follows an eight-step sequence:

1. Be warm, friendly, accepting, open, and honest.

2. Emphasize present behavior— "*What* are you doing?" *Why* is not important.

3. Insist on *value judgment.* Does what you are doing help you? Your class? Your school? Your home? Your community?

4. Plan better alternatives and make the plan feasible. ("Can you avoid fighting until noon?")

5. Get a commitment, either oral or written, from the student. If the commitment is written, get the student's signature.

6. Get feedback, and accept *no* excuses.

7. If necessary, get another, more viable commitment. Repeat, repeat, repeat, if necessary.

8. Do not punish.

COOPERATIVE LEARNING

Cooperative Learning is structured group activity in which students discover or master learning objectives.

By assuming specific roles (such as leader, recorder, reporter, or timekeeper), all students become actively engaged in the learning process. Teachers assess the extent to which objectives have been achieved on both an individual and a group level. Teachers can also assess how well students have learned the content as well as the development of social skills.

EXTRINISIC REWARDS

Experience and research have demonstrated that students are more likely to be motivated positively by the use of extrinsic rewards rather than by taking away privileges. For example, pupils who find it impossible to stay with the tasks of learning to read or learning to control their classroom behaviors under the traditional motivations (teacher, peer, or parent encouragement; approval, pressure, and punishment systems) *have* learned to read or behave better when rewarded with tokens: marbles, candy, toys, stars, emblems, titles, and so forth.

In addition to objects used as awards, privileges can be strong motivators. Short-term motivations may include free time or a longer recess or lunch period; longer-term procedures could include a cumulative point (or token) system that would lead to the privilege of attending movies or special field trips. The teacher *and* the students can work together to build a system based on a self-management sheet, listing mutually agreed upon important behaviors, such as punctuality, care of school property, completed assignments, courteousness, and so forth. (See Self-Management Record.)

FLEXIBLE SCHEDULING

Flexible scheduling was invented to increase educational effectiveness via the individualization of student instruction. Computer technology can deal with the complexities involved. For example, outstanding students can be released from "required" classes and provided with advanced texts and study materials, with only occasional contacts with the regular teacher. Students who need simpler materials and more time to learn can be taught effectively by older students or adult aides.

FLIGHT PLAN

The flight plan is an approach to lesson planning that evolved over the years through work with high-school, junior-high, and elementary-school students. The flight plan is an effort to personalize, as well as individualize, assignments in a manner that follows important learning principles.

The flight-plan approach, which is hierarchical, allows teachers to work as artist-technicians. First, they need to find out two things about a particular student: what does that student need to learn (to read better, to compute, to organize ideas), and what are his or her interests? This information enables the teacher to individualize instruction so that it is personally meaningful to the student.

Trained teachers have the skills to detect, via formal and informal means, the present level on which the student is functioning. Next, they must thoughtfully identify the learning objectives that students and teachers have as their common goals. Having done this, teachers must take a close look at the skills needed to

accomplish the goals. A good motto in lesson planning is "First things first," or as a good friend, J. Louis Cooper, used to say, "Remember, he can't jump high if he can't jump low!"

A format delineating the skeletal structure of the flight plan appears on page 264. It indicates the segments of the plan and briefly describes the emphasis on each level of operation. This format, or check board, includes four flights, but there can be more. The check board can be duplicated on a large board for planning purposes. For instance, after a teacher has the objectives clearly in mind and has identified the skills, he or she can use the box under Flight 1, Number 2, to make notes regarding the books, exercises, and so on that will be used in teaching the skills. As new ideas occur to the planner, he or she can make note of them, always being careful to put them in their logical place on the continuum.

The teacher duplicates the plan, one for each student. This way students know what is ahead and can plan accordingly. Evaluation is continuous, with the teacher or an aide usually in charge. The teacher makes parents aware of the plan and encourages them to become involved, particularly in Flights III and IV, which emphasize divergent thinking and creative activities.

A plan such as this incorporates certain safety measures. First, clear objectives make meaningless, isolated assignments virtually impossible; second, subsequent parts must be constructed so that they reinforce previous learnings; third, in systems that use letter-grade evaluations, the possibility of failure is eliminated because Flight I is equated with a grade of D, Flight II with a C, Flight III with a B,

A Flight-Plan Check Board

NAME OF CLASS OR INDIVIDUAL STUDENT _____

BEHAVIORAL OBJECTIVE _____

EMPHASIS	FLIGHT I: GROUND CREW WORK	FLIGHT II: THE TAKE-OFF	FLIGHT III: FLYING HIGH	FLIGHT IV: ON THE MOON
1. Who's in charge?	Teacher directs	Student works with teacher as helper	Student works with other student or alone	Student solos
2. What's the nature of the work?	*Basic*: skill drill	*Augmented*: skills application	*Divergent*: activities with many choices	*Culminating*: unique creative products and activities
3. How can the learnings be categorized?	Simple	Complex	Compound	Sophisticated
4. How can the learnings be described?	*Cognitively*: knowledge and comprehension *Affectively*: awareness and responding	Application Valuing	Analysis Organizing	Synthesis and evaluation Internalizing values
5. What are some titles of flights that will help the learner comprehend the natural sequences involved in every learning endeavor?	"The Egg" "The Overture" "Change: In General" "Change: In My Community"	"The Larva" "Opus I" "Change: In Me" "Change: In My State"	"The Pupa" "Opus II" "Change: In My School" "Change: In My Country"	"The Adult" "The finale" "Change: In My Neighborhood" "Change: In The World"

and Flight IV with an A, in systems that use letter-grade evaluations. Being relieved of the possibility of failure is a great motivator!

The flights may be long and involved or extremely brief and simple. In either case, the principle is the same. From the incubation stage the learnings unfold until there is a resultant creative product. This mode of planning may encourage a teacher to combine and recombine old and new methods so that teaching remains vital and both teacher and students continue to enjoy learning.

INQUIRY PROCESS

The inquiry process in learning is designed to maximize the student's capabilities in learning a new concept. Closely allied to "discovery technique" and "the divergent thinking strategy," it can be applied as easily to a student's learning about his or her own behavior and its modification as to academic conceptualizations. The key lies in a teacher's skill in questioning. Nonthreatening, matter-of-fact questions will be most productive when the teacher (1) isolates the elements of the situation, (2) devises hypotheses about the elements, (3) pursues what might be true (consequences) if the hypotheses were correct, (4) keeps the whole situation in mind, and not only isolated aspects, (5) considers, accepts, and rejects a variety of possibilities, and (6) comes to conclusions by thinking about the thoughts developed during steps 1 through 5.

A teacher's questions could well pursue the following areas, from the simple to the complex: sensory observations; recalling; comparing-contrasting; classifying-grouping; analyzing; interpreting; inferring; generalizing; hypothesizing; predicting; evaluating—value judging; synthesizing.

LEARNING STYLES

Learning styles are the biological, sociological, and psychological elements that determine how students learn best. Learning styles are characterized by perceptual modalities (visual, auditory, tactile/kinesthetic), grouping arrangements, and global (big picture) versus analytic (detail) approaches to integrating new information. Studies show that matched learning and teaching styles enhance student success in learning.

Teachers and parents interested in learning more about practical applications of research in the area of learning styles will find helpful information in the textbook *Student Learning Styles* published by the National Association of Secondary School Principals, 1904 Association Drive, Reston, VA 22091. Selected references in this book also contain information about learning.

LEGAL-TYPE NOTE-TAKING

Legal-type note-taking is somewhat imitative of legal briefs. The approach is very simple. Instead of using traditional outline format or hit-or-miss note taking, this method sticks to questions and answers. Preferably, one section of a notebook is allocated for a given subject. To implement this kind of note-taking, have the student:

1. Begin by opening the notebook to the second page. At the top of the left-hand page write "class notes." On the opposite page write "reading notes."

2. Under "reading notes," write the name of the subject, the chapter number, and the date.

3. Take a ruler and draw a line down the center of the page on the right. At the top of the first column write "question"; at the top of the second column write "answer."

4. Begin reading the text. Each paragraph should contain one or two main ideas worth remembering. Identify the significant fact or idea.

5. Now convert that fact or idea into a question. (If a student can't do that, he or she may not understand the material.) Formulate the question in as brief a form as possible, and after number 1, write it out. On the other side of the center line place another 1, followed by the answer in very brief form. Keep the numbers in line with each other down the page. See the sample below.

The left-hand page is free for class notes during the teacher's lecture, a student's report, or slide or transparency showings. Draw arrows from your notes to the diagrams or reminders, and vice versa. Remember, reinforcement of ideas enhances learning.

This method of note taking is especially helpful when reviewing for exams. A friend or a relative can ask the questions from the notebook and the answers are right there; no need for time-consuming hunting for the answers. And, the notebook may come in handy even after a class is finished.

LISTENING FORMULA

The FALR formula for listening has been very useful for a large number of students. The letters refer to

1. *F*ocusing attention on the speaker.

2. *A*sking what might or should be learned from the speaker.

3. *L*istening carefully, all the while relating new material to what is already known about the subject. Listen for the main ideas, key words, particular points of interest.

4. *R*eviewing what has been learned in the way that works best, perhaps by making notes for future reference, relating new ideas to a friend, or pursuing the subject through independent study.

LEGAL-TYPE NOTE-TAKING

CLASS NOTES

Place here any pertinent teacher's notes; reminders for tomorrow; new assignment; diagrams.

READING NOTES

Biology
Chapter 8   DATE _____

QUESTION   ANSWER

1. What was . . . .   1. xmxmxmx xmx
. . . .?   xx x x xxxxxxx

2.   2.

266

MAINSTREAMING/INCLUSION

Mainstreaming and inclusion refer to a system whereby students with special needs are placed in regular classes with regular educational expectations. In response to Public Law-94-142, often known as IDEA - Individuals with Disabilities Education Act (least restrictive environment), students are mainstreamed whenever possible. The appropriateness of a student's placement is determined by the extent to which the student can handle mainstream expectations with some accommodations.

Inclusion refers to a student with special needs being placed in a regular education class for purposes of socialization. The teacher may or may not assign a grade, and the student may be accompanied by an adult teacher's aide, if required by the student's IEP (Individualized Education Plan). Inclusion also exposes "normal" children to those with disabilities. Familiarity and regular interactions between students with and without disabilities may aid normal interactions outside of school and in society at large.

MEDIATION

The word "mediation" has crept into the everyday conversation of many students, particularly those with parents involved in divorce or settlement proceedings. Simply put, mediation is a way of resolving problems that don't belong in the courtroom or a therapist's office.

While it is true that mediation is being used increasingly in divorce proceedings, it is not limited to those. The technique is being used for all types of conflict, such as coping with troublesome neighbors, aging parents, or parents in multiple marriages with several sets of children.

Mediators (*not* arbitrators) do not tell people what to do, but they assist the interested parties in coming to terms. They are neutral participants, primarily interested in aiding people to agree on decisions about conflicts in an effort to chart their plans. The goal of a mediator is to help solve problems amicably rather than adversarily.

The mediation process directly involves students in the settlement of disputes. Students are informed about the availability of mediators and how they work. For instance, the students indicate whether they would prefer mediation to resolution by a school faculty member. If they agree to mediate, they are asked to respect their adversary by *listening* without interruption, *refraining* from name calling, *pledging* to be truthful, *offering* possible solutions to the problem, and *carrying out* the agreed-upon plan.

ORGANIZING A CLASSROOM

Students learn best when they feel that they have some control over their own learning. When students are empowered, they feel that they own the process as well as the product of their own work. A classroom should belong to both the students and the teacher. Whether the students are in a room for only one period or for the entire day, it should be a place they look forward to entering. This feeling or attitude may not be achieved, particularly on the upper elementary level, if the teacher has everything lined up, neat and orderly, when the students arrive.

Instead, a teacher may have on hand a rich collection of materials: textbooks, library books, paperbacks, reference books, old and new magazines, puzzles, games, furniture that no one else wanted, paper, paints, scissors, string, and junk. Students who are used to a more structured environment may think they are in the wrong room, but they will soon get to work on organizing the room as they think best.

Once students are comfortable, they will begin to work together, establishing priorities as a group. Leadership will emerge and imaginations will take flight. The students will, of course, bring their previous class organization ideas with them, but given latitude they are almost certain to want to create something entirely different from anything they've had before. If students opt to try the same old thing they've had in another school, the teacher should go along with it for the time being. He or she should stand back and watch, listen, help when needed, and step in, if necessary; after all, he or she is a member of this group, not an onlooker.

There will be some competition for stimulating creative ways to solve problems, but sooner or later students will see the need for some management. Perhaps they will want to choose leaders or officers. All the while they are working through ways to make their room the most interesting one in the school, they are putting the books in order, sorting the supplies, getting to know each other. And this is an excellent opportunity for students to use math skills, as in plotting the arrangement of the furniture using graph paper.

As all of this is happening, the teacher can closely observe the kinds of books the students pick up and mull over, the level of book that they stay with, their preferences in friends, their dexterity, their voices, their attitudes toward one another, and their feelings about themselves. Students may even make lists of things they want to accomplish before the year is over. The teacher's goals and students' goals may be in sync because all class members were given the opportunity to help structure their environment.

PEER MENTORS/LEADERSHIP TRAINING (JUNIOR COUNSELORS)

A leadership training program enlists the aid of students to help their peers. Teachers can recommend students for training to prepare them to work with individuals and small groups. The trainees might meet regularly prior to the opening of school. During that time they can explore the differences among democratic, autocratic, and *laissez-faire* procedures. They can examine the roles they themselves habitually assumed in groups (interrogator, clarifier, antagonist, peace maker, and so on). They can also study active listening, questioning and clarification techniques, and regard for confidentialities.

Peer mentors may not only assume the role of confidante and helper to individuals and small groups who have problems with study habits, academic and social skills, truancy, and loneliness, but they may also assist in the total orientation program of the school. Members of a successful program may infuse the entire school with an atmosphere of friendliness and good will. At the end of the year they might be awarded a small token of recognition for their accomplishments. However, with luck students may realize that the satisfaction of helping others help themselves can be their highest reward.

QUESTIONNAIRE

The questionnaire is a widely used technique for collecting information or statistical data. Filling out a questionnaire allows students an opportunity for introspection. Some of the information may be shared with classmates to help students get to know each other. There are many samples in professional books and periodicals; others can be purchased..

When working with children on a particular problem in school, adaptations or self-made questionnaires have distinct advantages. First, they will be relevant—the children use their own topics and terminology. Second, the purposes and meanings become clear to the users. Third, there is pride in "something that is mine."

A questionnaire "About Me" might include such questions as: What are the names and ages of my brothers and sisters? What are the names of my three best friends? What do I do when I have time to do as I please? Do I listen to the radio? When? What are my favorite musical groups? Do I watch TV? When? What are my favorite programs? What hobby do I have? Which subjects in school do I like best? If I could be granted three wishes, what would they be?

ROLE PLAYING

In role playing, pupils reenact behavior episodes for the purpose of studying their own behavior and learning

how to control it. For example, suppose two pupils want a single copy of a book at the same time, and conflict results in physical blows. After the teacher resolves the immediate conflict and the emotion has subsided, the pupils may change roles or other pupils may play one or both of the roles to reenact the conflict from its beginning, recalling as nearly as possible the words and actions of the episode. The class can then discuss why the conflict took place.

When the motivations and causes of the conflict seem to be defined, the entire class can offer suggestions as to how the conflict could have been avoided by another way of behaving. Then the two students are given an opportunity to practice the new way of behaving.

SELF-MANAGEMENT RECORD

A self-management record is a useful tool for identifying classroom behaviors and alerting the students to important considerations when interacting with one another. The items listed on the sample (see page 270) relate to responsibility and integrity. However, teachers and students may tailor a self-management record to meet their specific expectations and goals. Periodic checks readily reflect changes in conduct. For the student, the list forces some self-evaluation; for the teacher, the record is useful when counseling a student, talking with a parent, and determining citizenship marks.

SENTENCE COMPLETION

The sentence completion technique is a procedure in which the teacher and

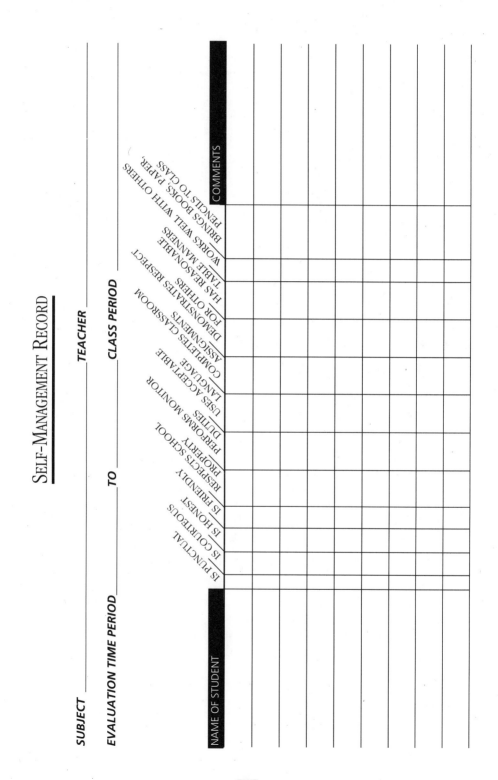

SELF-MANAGEMENT RECORD

SUBJECT _____

TEACHER _____

EVALUATION TIME PERIOD _____ TO _____ CLASS PERIOD _____

NAME OF STUDENT	IS PUNCTUAL	IS COURTEOUS	IS HONEST	IS FRIENDLY	RESPECTS SCHOOL PROPERTY	PERFORMS MONITOR DUTIES	USES ACCEPTABLE LANGUAGE	COMPLETES CLASSROOM ASSIGNMENTS	DEMONSTRATES RESPECT FOR OTHERS	HAS REASONABLE TABLE MANNERS	WORKS WELL WITH OTHERS	BRINGS BOOKS, PAPER, PENCILS TO CLASS	COMMENTS

a student may learn about the latter's attitudes toward specific people, relationships, and experiences. This technique can be designed to elicit a student's feelings toward school, work, play, authority figures, joys, and fears. Forms are available from test publishers, or teachers may develop their own by using a variety of structures. Examples of sentence completion items include:

I feel _____
Teachers are _____
My problem is _____
I dislike _____
My father's greatest mistake was

_____
Mary is _____
The fight was _____
The situation is _____

STAFF MEETING

The staff meeting is a regularized procedure designed to provide optimal help for a teacher and a student. Teachers and administrators of a school select a common meeting time when special-service personnel (counselors, nurse, psychologist, special education teacher, and so on) meet with an administrator and any teacher(s) concerned about the developmental behavior of a particular student. The agenda comes from teacher, parent, or special-service personnel concerns. All participants receive a copy of the agenda in staff mailboxes prior to the meeting so that all who want to help may come prepared. Participants share data and agree on an action plan. The plan includes follow-up strategies. This procedure works best when meetings are held *regularly.*

STUDY SKILLS

There are specific study skills that any teacher can teach to any student. The following guidelines are taken from Myrtle T. Collins' *How to Study* (Big Spring, Texas: Gamco Industries, 1972).

1. Don't study on an empty stomach—or on one that is too full.
2. Have your vision checked once a year.
3. Learn to listen (see Listening Formula).
4. Take a diagnostic test; then improve your reading.
5. Use the following SQ4R study formula; Scan, Question, Read, Review, Recite, Reinforce.
6. Learn to concentrate.
7. Make a daily activity schedule.
8. Identify the time of day you work best.
9. Select the same quiet, neat place to study daily.
10. Take good notes.
11. Use loose-leaf dividers.
12. Give yourself lots of time to prepare for examinations.
13. Reward yourself for jobs well done.

Active Parenting. 45 video vignettes. Marietta, GA: Active Parenting, Inc., (currently being revised).

> The vignettes present a series of situations that show how to help children by using principles of cooperation, encouragement, and responsibility.

Amatea, Ellen S. Brief *Strategic Intervention for School Behavior Problems.* San Francisco: Jossey-Bass, 1989.

> The author presents a practical, step-by-step guide for resolving persistent school behavior problems.

Barth, Roland S. *Improving School from Within.* San Francisco: Jossey-Bass, 1990.

> This author's philosophy is that teachers who are leaders promote growth in their students. A collaborative system, a community of leaders, enlists all members to make important contributions toward growth.

Caine, Renate Nummela, and Caine, Geoffrey. *Making Connections: Teaching and the Human Brain.* Alexandria, VA: Association for Supervision and Curriculum Development, 1991.

> The Caines examine education in light of new research regarding the functioning of the brain. The research is related to current educational and curricular issues and, specifically, to enhancing learning.

Capuzzi, Dave, and Gross, Douglas R. *Youth at Risk: A Resource for Counselors, Teachers, and Parents.* Alexandria, VA: American Association for Counseling and Development, 1989.

> The authors provide dozens of techniques for helping prevent and treat problems such as eating disorders, suicide, drug abuse, and dropping out of school.

Cline, Foster, and Fay, Jim. *Parenting with Love and Logic.* Colorado Springs, CO: NavPress, 1990.

> This book focuses on teaching children responsibility through practice as well as on learning the logic of life through problem solving. It details a win-win approach to parenting.

Fairchild, Thomas N. *Crisis Intervention Strategies for School-Based Helpers.* Springfield, IL: Charles C. Thomas, 1989.

> Fairchild details prevention and intervention strategies for family problems, abuse and neglect, substance abuse, grief, violent behavior, suicide, eating disorders, pregnancy, and stress.

"Friends" Raping Friends: Could It Happen to You? Washington, DC: Center for Women's Policy Studies, 1987.

> This booklet presents case studies and rape prevention strategies. It explains how families can help the victim, and it includes information on the legal implications of sexual assault.

Gall, M. D.; Gall, Joyce; Jacobsen, Dennis R.; and Bullock, Terry. *Tools for Learning: A Guide to Teaching Study Skills.* Alexandria, VA: Association for Supervision and Curriculum Development, 1990.

> The authors provide practical information on important study skills and describe how to teach them. They also summarize research on various aspects of study skills instruction.

Glasser, William, M.D. *The Quality School: Managing Students without Coercion.* New York: Harper & Row, 1990.

> Dr. Glasser speaks directly about establishing a quality school in a non-coercive, lead-management environment. He relates classroom instruction to extra-curricular activities in terms of engaging students in the learning process.

Golden, Larry B., and Capuzzi, Dave. *Helping Families Help Children.* Springfield, IL: Charles C. Thomas, 1987.

> This book describes a process for family involvement in resolving student behavior problems in school.

Hughes, Della. "Running Away: A 50-50 Chance to Survive?" *USA TODAY* 118: 64-66, 1989.

> Hughes provides recent statistics on runaway teens as well as anecdotal evidence on how runaways live. She also includes concrete suggestions and alternatives to help runaways.

Johnson, S. W., and Maile, L. J. *Suicide and the Schools.* Springfield, IL: Charles C. Thomas, 1987.

> The authors present information about how to recognize an impending problem, how to work with the student who has attempted suicide, and how to help survivors in the school.

Kain, Craig D. *No Longer Immune: A Guide to AIDS.* Alexandria, VA: American Association for Counseling and Development, 1989.

> Putting the disease in practical terms, this book provides techniques for helping people cope with AIDS.

Kremer, B., and Farnum, M. "Dropouts, Absentees and Illinois Education Policy." *Illinois Association for Counseling and Development Quarterly* 97: 19-26, 1985.

> The authors provide a good look at what needs to be done to curb the drop-out rate in our schools.

Kubler-Ross, E. *On Children and Death*. New York: Macmillan, 1983.
> This book provides a clear explanation of how a child views death.

Molnar, Alex, and Lindquist, Barbara. *Changing Problem Behavior in Schools*. San Francisco: Jossey-Bass, 1989.
> Molnar and Lindquist offer specific methods for promoting positive change in student behavior.

Moschetti-Houff, Clayton. "Introduction to the Twelve Steps." *Adolescent Counselor* 1:23-25, April-May, 1988.
> The twelve steps that have helped millions recover from various types of addictions are explained and presented in a pull-out section.

Orten, J. D., and Soll, S. K., "Runaway Children and Their Families: A Treatment Typology." *Journal of Family Issues* 1:249-261, 1980.
> This article analyzes the development of the runaway problem and the dramatic increases in the number of runaways.

Palker, P. "How to Deal with the Single-Parent Child in the Classroom." *Teacher* 98: 50-54, 1980.
> Information in this article helps the teacher to be sensitive to and to avoid stigmatizing children of single-parent families.

Quinett, Paul G. Suicide: *The Forever Decision*. New York: Continuum, 1988.
> For those considering suicide, this book offers credible arguments for holding on. For their families and friends, it offers a window into the despairing mind, perhaps in time to arouse life-saving concern.

Rosemond, John. *Ending the Homework Hassle*. Kansas City, MO: Andrews and McMeel, 1990.
> This helpful book aids parents in disengaging themselves from homework hassles as they guide their children toward success in school.

Ruggerio, Ryan. *Saving Your Child's Mind*. Springfield, IL: Charles C. Thomas, 1988.
> The author provides easy-to-implement strategies to motivate children to learn, to develop creative and thinking skills, to make moral judgments, and to achieve excellence in written and spoken expression.

Sensor, M. C. *Stress Management for Children and Adolescents*. Des Moines: Iowa Department of Public Instruction, 1986.
> Based on the Mathews Stress Management Model, this book gives specific techniques for counselors and teachers to enable students to cope with stress.

Sexual Assault Education and Prevention Project and Women's Center of Northwestern University. *Breaking the Silence: What You Should Know About Sexual Assault. A Guide for Women and Men*. Evanston, IL: Northwestern University, 1990.

> This pamphlet provides valuable information about how to prevent sexual assault. It also gives specific measures for what to do, for both victims and others, after an assault has taken place.

Sexually Transmitted Diseases: How to Recognize Them, How to Treat Them, How to Prevent Them. Daly City, CA: Krames Communications, 1986.

> This pamphlet dispels myths and presents facts about sexually transmitted diseases in precise, understandable terms.

Sonbuchner, Gail Murphy. *Help Yourself: How to Take Advantage of Your Learning Styles*. Syracuse, NY: New Readers Press, 1991.

> The author defines learning styles and provides a number of inventories that help readers discover personal learning strengths and weaknesses. The book also contains specific techniques for helping students organize themselves for learning and to remember and integrate information.

Sunburst Communications. *Videocassettes and Filmstrips*. Pleasantville, NY: Sunburst Communications, current.

> These prize-winning visual aids focus on topics of health, drug education, personal development, and coping with crises.

U. S. Department of Education. *AIDS and the Education of Our Children*. Washington, DC: United States Department of Education, 1988.

> This concise and helpful handbook, written by former Secretary of Education William J. Bennett and his staff, answers such questions as: What is AIDS? How is the HIV virus transmitted? How are adolescents at risk of contracting AIDS? What can be done? The authors specifically address the issue of children with AIDS in the schools and give appropriate actions for school personnel.

Wood, George H. *Schools that Work*. New York: Dutton, 1992.

> The author takes the reader into schools around the United States and shows the elements that make the difference between schools that work and schools that do not.

P

Paranoia, 173
  See also Health Problems

Passive behavior, 174-175
  See also Attention seeking;
  Fearfulness

Peer mentors/leadership training
(junior counselors), 268-269

Physical differences, 175-177
  See also Health problems;
  Self-concept

Pornography, 177

Prejudice, 178
  See also Bilingual children;
  Multicultural population

Pre-vacation syndrome, 179
  See also Hyperactivity

Procrastination, 180-181
  See also Anxiety; Homework;
  Self-concept; Study skills

Q

Questionnaire, 269

R

Reading problems, 182-183
  See also Disabilities, learning;
  Study skills

Rejected children, 184-185
  See also Loneliness; Self-concept;
  Sibling Rivalry

Religious reasons, for absences, 4

Restlessness, 186-187
  See also Anxiety; Wanderers

Role playing, 269

Rudeness, 187-188

Runaways, 188-189
  See also Dropouts; Potential stress

S

School phobia, 190-191
  See also Anxiety; Fearfulness

Self-concept, 192-193
  See also Ashamed students;
  Underachievers

Self-management record, 269, 270

Sentence completion, 269, 271

Sexual assault, 193-195
  See also Abused children; AIDS;
  Exhibitionism; Health problems;
  Masturbation

Sexually transmitted diseases
(STDs), 195-196
  See also AIDS

Sibling rivalry, 197-198
  See also Jealousy; Twins

Slam books, 199-200

Slow learners, 200-201
  See also Disabilities, learning;
  Self-concept

Smoking, 202-203

Soiling, 203-204
  See also Anxiety

Speech problems, 204-205
  See also Stuttering

Staff meeting, 271

Stealing, 206-208
  See also Immoral behavior; Lying

Stepchildren, 208-209
  See also Changing family structure;
  Stress

Stress, 210-211
  See also Anxiety; Drug use;
  Jealousy

Stubbornness, 212-213
  See also Argumentativeness;
  Compulsiveness; Fearfulness;
  Maturational delay

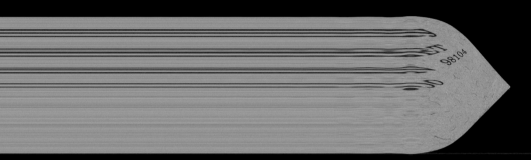

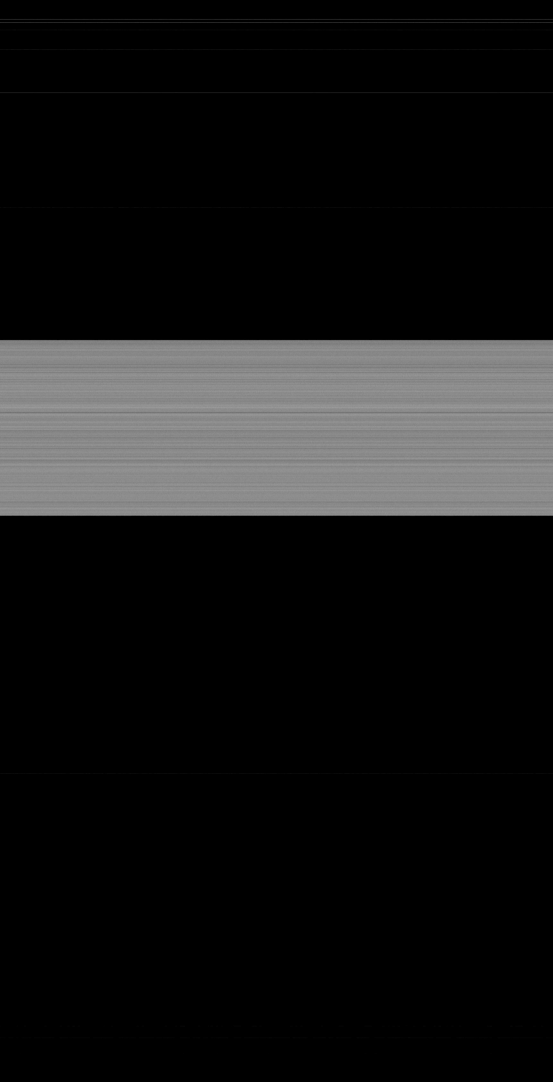